DEDICATION

The late Milton Richman, for many years Sports Editor of United Press International, was a great friend and supporter of Little League. He was also a special friend to me during the years I was a college journalism student and worked for United Press. Milt wrote lovingly of Little League and taught me a great deal about how to write. On behalf of Little League Baseball and myself, therefore, this book is dedicated to his memory.

GROWING UP AT BAT

50 Years of Little League Baseball®

ALSO BY HARVEY FROMMER

Throwing Heat: Autobiography of Nolan Ryan
Primitive Baseball: The National Pastime in the Gilded Age
150th Anniversary Album of Baseball
Red on Red: Autobiography of Red Holzman
Olympic Controversies
City Tech: The First Forty Years
Baseball's Greatest Managers
Baseball's Hall of Fame
Games of the XXIII Olympiad 1984 Commemorative Book
Jackie Robinson
Baseball's Greatest Records, Streaks & Feats
Sports Genes
Baseball's Greatest Rivalry: The New York Yankees and the Boston Red Sox
Rickey and Robinson: The Men Who Broke Baseball's Color Line
Basketball My Way: Nancy Lieberman
The Sports Date Book
New York City Baseball: The Last Golden Age 1947-1957
The Great American Soccer Book
Sports Roots
Sports Lingo: A Dictionary of the Language of Sports
The Martial Arts: Judo and Karate
A Sailing Primer
A Baseball Century: The First Hundred Years of the National League

50 Years of Little League Baseball®

GROWING UP AT BAT

HARVEY FROMMER

PHAROS BOOKS
A SCRIPPS HOWARD COMPANY
NEW YORK

Pharos Books are available at special discounts on bulk purchases for sales promotions, premi ums, fundraising or educational use. For details, contact the Special Sales Department, Pharos Books, 200 Park Avenue, New York, NY 10166.

Cover and text design: Nancy Eato
Cover photography by Arthur Krasinsky
Interior photos courtesy of Little League Baseball, Inc. and Vannucci Foto-Services, Williamsport, Pa.

Copyright © 1989 by Harvey Frommer
and Little League Baseball, Incorporated.

All rights reserved. No part of this book may be reproduced in any form or by any means without written permission of the publisher.

First published in 1989.

Library of Congress Cataloging-in-Publication Data

Frommer, Harvey.
Growing up at bat : fifty years of
Little League Baseball/Harvey Frommer;
introduction by A. Bartlett Giamatti.
p. cm.
Includes index.
ISBN 0-88687-439-4 : $24.95. --
ISBN 0-88687-419-X (pbk.) : $12.95
1. Little League Baseball, inc.--
History. I. Title.
GV880.5.F76 1989 88-34324
796.357'62--dc19 CIP

Pharos ISBN 0-88687-419-X

Printed in the United States of America

Pharos Books
A Scripps Howard Company
200 Park Avenue
New York, NY 10166

10 9 8 7 6 5 4 3 2 1

CONTENTS

ACKNOWLEDGMENTS

This book was written under a great deal of pressure in a very compressed time frame. It would never have been completed without the help given by my wife, Myrna Frommer. She helped organize, edit, and write the manuscript. So, in any list of acknowledgments, she belongs at the very top.

Others who gave of their time and memories, and to whom I am indebted, included Dr. Creighton Hale, Bob Wirz, Steve Keener, Tim Hughes, Dr. Luke Laporta, Frank Rizzo, Ray Keyes, John Lindemuth, Beverly Gray, Irv Kaze, Bill Shea, Dr. Robert Yasui, Arnold White, the Baseball Hall of Fame, and the kind folks at the Peter J. McGovern Little League Museum. I extend a special thank-you to all the interviewees.

Lastly, my thanks to Hana Lane, editor-in-chief at Pharos, and David Hendin. They were wonderful people to work with.

INTRODUCTION

Little League Baseball has been ours for the past fifty years. A sport and a program, a way of life and a style of living, a quest and a fulfillment, it is in the fabric of millions of lives and dreams.

Nurtured and supported by dedicated volunteers, joyously pursued by players and their families, the game that began that long-ago summer's day in 1939 in Williamsport, Pennsylvania, is now an international phenomenon.

Little League Baseball embodies some of the truly good things we have as a society: honest competition, democratic participation and teamwork, clear structure and defined roles. And although not all those who play the game are winners when the final score is tallied, all win through their participation in this most enchanting of sports for youth.

The players through the years have literally been "growing up at bat." From their first tentative steps and swings in T-ball; through interaction with other players, with coaches and managers; through seasons at the higher levels of organized competition, boys and girls grow into adulthood aided and enhanced by lessons on the playing fields of Little League Baseball.

Although Little League Baseball was not designed to be a feeder program for organized baseball, happily it has worked out to be just that. More than two-thirds of current-day major leaguers once played Little League Baseball. And for the big leaguers, the diamonds of their youth they dreamed on still make the past for them as real as the present. All are quick enthusiastically to reminisce about what Little League meant to them. Such memories are real not only for major leaguers, but also for the millions of others around the world who still remember their days of Little League Baseball.

Thus it is significant that *Growing Up at Bat: 50 Years of Little League Baseball* is now part of the library of baseball books. A celebration and a memento, a history and a montage of memories, this book will have a prominent place on my bookshelf and serve as a reminder of the five decades of accomplishment of the Little League Baseball program and its important role in the history of the national pastime.

A. BARTLETT GIAMATTI

50 Years of Little League Baseball®

Lycoming

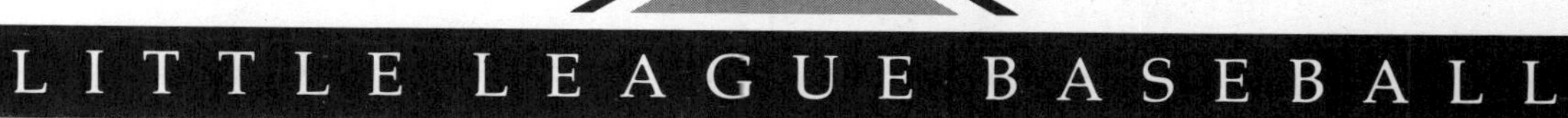

The Beginnings

In the sun that is young once only,
Time let me play and be
Golden in the mercy of his means. . . .

Dylan Thomas, "Fern Hill"

The fateful summer of 1939 the United States tarried a while in innocence. The world was poised on the precipice of all-out war. In Europe the sounds of angry oratory fused with the roar of armies readying to face the terror of mortal combat. But in America martial sounds were limited to the spirited drumbeats of Decoration Day parades and the crack of Fourth of July fireworks.

That America of 1939 was a nation of small towns where baseball was—as it had been for a century—the summer game. The sport's centennial was celebrated that summer. And the Baseball Hall of Fame was dedicated in Cooperstown—a historic village near the source of the Susquehanna River in upstate New York.

Some hundreds of miles to the southwest that same river flows through Williamsport, Pennsylvania, a small town in the shadow of the Allegheny Mountains. There a young man who worked at the local sandpaper plant had an idea about giving the young boys in his town a chance to play real baseball.

As a youth, Carl Stotz was often shunted off to the sidelines by older boys when they played baseball. Now his neph-

Carl Stotz originated the idea for Little League Baseball to give his nephews Harold "Major" Gehron, aged eight, and Jimmy Gehron, aged six, a chance to play organized baseball.

ews, Jimmy and Harold "Major" Gehron, aged six and eight, were complaining that they weren't allowed into any organized baseball games, and the twenty-nine-year-old Stotz remembered how he felt when he was kept out. He thought of a way to make it possible for his nephews to play.

Stotz, known to his nephews as "Uncle Tuck," said (the story goes), "I have an idea to get you boys into organized baseball. How would you like to play on a regular team, with uniforms, a new ball for every game and bats you can really swing?"

"Who would we play?" the nephews asked. "Where would we get the uniforms and balls and bats? Would anybody come around to see us play?"

"Don't worry," Uncle Tuck told Jimmy and Major. "I'll work out a plan for a league. You'll wear store-bought suits and play on a real diamond."

The low-keyed but determined Stotz was true to his word. Lacking a background in organized athletics, he brought his idea to Bert and George Bebble, Williamsport brothers who had once played semi-pro baseball. The Bebbles enthusiastically joined with Stotz in the task of creating what would become Little League Baseball. They organized a three-team league of thirty boys. Stotz and the Bebble brothers would each manage a team.

The idea of Little League Baseball was simple yet inspired. The national pastime had

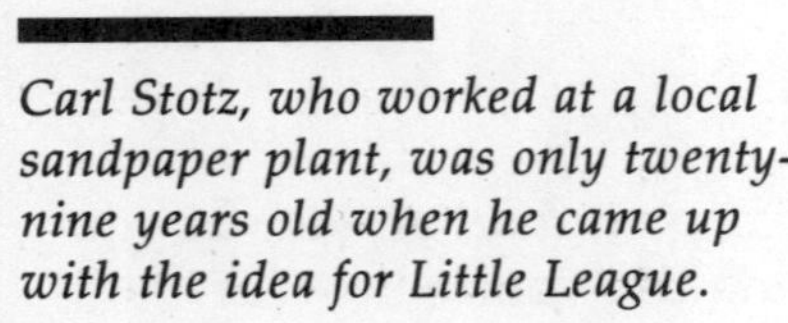

Carl Stotz, who worked at a local sandpaper plant, was only twenty-nine years old when he came up with the idea for Little League.

Only three teams, thirty boys in all, played in the Little League in 1939, its first year. They were the Lycoming Dairy Farms team, the Jumbo Pretzel Company team, and the Lundy Lumber team. This team photo montage was the handiwork of Carl Stotz.

been around for a century, but in its organized form it was almost exclusively reserved for teenagers and adults. In the main, it was off limits for young children. But now the boys of Williamsport aged eight to twelve would be able to play on a scaled-down field. There would be good playing conditions, adult supervision, and no threat of rejection by older boys.

Carl Stotz suggested getting community support for the program, a unique idea for that era. His plan was to solicit local merchants to sponsor the three teams. For a thirty-dollar contribution sponsors could have the name of their business sewn on the uniforms—Stotz's sole concession to any form of commercialization. He approached fifty-six merchants and, in his words, "had to do a lot of hard talking" before he was able to secure the first sponsor of a Little League team—the Lycoming Dairy. Lundy Lumber and Jumbo Pretzel soon followed.

Cooperation was the cornerstone of the program. Playing suits were purchased for $1.58 each at a chain store. Mothers sewed the lettering on the makeshift uniforms. The three

Howard Gair, who umpired the first game, remembered standing behind the pitcher to call balls and strikes.

teams would share eight baseball gloves and one $1.67 catcher's mask. The original bases were cheap duck material stuffed with wood shavings used for packing, donated by Flanagan's Drug Store. Later that same first season, mothers made replacement bases out of old feed bags that they filled with straw.

The first game was played on June 6, 1939. Lundy Lumber faced Lycoming Dairy on the field of a sandpaper plant on Memorial Avenue near Oliver Street west of Williamsport. A small news article in the next day's *Williamsport Sun* gave this report of the first game in the history of Little League Baseball:

Lundy staged two big innings to defeat Dairy in the Little League opener last evening. In a game filled with excitement for both fans and players, Sipe, hurling for Lundy, held the Lycoming batters in check and was in danger at no time in the game. Not until the third inning after Gehron relieved Miller in the box, were the Dairy boys able to quiet the bats of the Lundy sluggers, and from that point on the game developed into a close contest.

The score:

Lycoming Dairy 1 0 0 3 3 1 - 8
Lundy Lumber 7 8 4 2 2 0 - 23

Thursday evening Jumbo Pretzels will meet Lycoming Dairy and determine whether stage-fright prevented the Dairy boys from playing a better brand of ball.

The first Little League season was under way. It was a primitive affair of three teams playing twenty-four games on makeshift fields and town playgrounds. Carl Stotz kept a small slate blackboard in the trunk of his car. He would take this portable "scoreboard" to games and painstakingly chalk in the scores inning by inning.

"We had the rules printed on sheets of paper," recalled the late Howard Gair, the umpire in that first game, who remembered standing behind the pitcher (the normal position used in Little League at that time) to call balls and strikes. "Rules governing play came from professional baseball. Soon those sheets became torn, even lost.

We had to keep replacing them, but we knew Little League Baseball was an idea that had come to stay."

Fifty years later the key principles established that summer of 1939 still govern:

- The name remains Little League Baseball.
- The basic unit of organization is still the league and not the teams comprising the league.
- A playing field is still scaled down to two-thirds regulation size; the distance between the pitcher's mound and home plate is reduced to 46 feet.
- The unique system of selecting players from a common pool of players from well-defined geographic areas still exists.
- Player selection remains without regard to race, color, or creed, or sex.
- A given number of players in each of three age groups is still placed on each team.
- All funds contributed by sponsors are still placed in a common treasury for the equal benefit of each team.
- Exploitation by commercial interests is still not permitted

Fifty years later, the key principles established in 1939 for Little League still govern, including a distance of 46 feet between home plate (shown here in a 1939 photo) and the pitcher's mound.

Affable and gentlemanly, always dressed in a well-starched shirt and neatly pressed suit, Ray Keyes was the sports editor of the *Williamsport Sun-Gazette*, one of the oldest newspapers in the United States. Keyes was an office boy for the *Gazette* in 1939 at the start of what would become a lifelong love affair with journalism and Little League. Recalling how he posted that first season's scores on the outside wall of the newspaper building for passersby to see, Keyes savored the images of that time.

"The boys wore flannel uniforms. Their pants were always baggy, and sweatshirt sleeves stuck out from under their shirts. Some were gangly and uncoordinated. But," Keyes added, "there was a spirit. . . ."

The following year, Stotz enlisted an additional manager for the fledgling program. Silver-haired and genial, John Lindemuth recalled his Little League

experiences as he sat in the living room of his picture-book country cottage surrounded by a collection of clocks of all styles and sizes that chimed, struck, cuckooed, and played melodies on the hour. "Carl Stotz and I had gone to school together. So we knew each other a long time. One day he came over and asked if I'd like to manage one of the teams. You know how those things are—I stayed on for seventeen years.

"When I came on board that 1940 season," continued Lindemuth, "fathers pitched in and energetically cleared two hundred trees to create a new playing field at the corner of Demerest and Memorial Avenue."

"Williamsport was a small town," noted Ray Keyes, "but it had a great tradition of baseball throughout the twentieth century. We always had a Double A professional baseball team and gave it good support. There has always been a lot of community spirit in Williamsport."

For collections to raise money a Williamsport man designed a sturdy tin cup with one handle that was passed around at games with quite a degree of success during those early years. Many enjoyed a good-natured laugh when a shy youngster asked a spectator: "Would you please put something in the cup for the offering?"

Carl Stotz sensed the need for effective organization as Little League spread to surrounding communities. He was also sensitive to the program being dominated by large geographic areas and population centers where there was a bigger pool of players to draw from. "He organized the program along the lines of school-zone districts," said Lindemuth. "No more than fifteen thousand people could reside in a Little League district. [Today this limit has been enlarged to 20,000.] In this way, no one geographical region could be dominant. The plan also helped Little League to grow.

"Williamsport had a league," Lindemuth continued, "but the boys in the lower end of Newberry couldn't play there, so they had to organize their own league. The other sections followed. And that's how Little League Baseball spread across Pennsylvania and all over—along district lines."

During World War II, Little League programs began in towns throughout Pennsylvania. A second league was formed in Williamsport—the Maynard Midgets. Teams now used canvas uniforms: no flannel was available for civilian use because of wartime demands. Proper equipment was a constant problem during those early Little League years—no one had ever manufactured bats, bases, or uniforms designed with the safety needs of children in mind.

As Little League Baseball evolved, all types of people became involved. They ranged from the man known as "Mr. Baseball"—Connie Mack—to an army of volunteers who would become the backbone of the program. Baseball legend Connie Mack, who would become the first of many major league boosters of the sport, came to Williamsport in 1944. He was highly impressed with what he saw.

"It would not surprise me one bit," the patrician Mack observed, "if some of these boys playing Little League Baseball made the major leagues"—prophetic words. Joey Jay was twelve years old in 1948 when the Little League program came to his home town of Middletown, Connecticut. Five years later Jay would be a member of the Milwaukee Braves, the first Little Leaguer to make the major leagues.

While Mack was steeped in baseball lore and therefore had a natural interest in youngsters playing the game, others with no familiarity with the national pastime became enamored of and entwined with Little League.

During the war years, English-born Bill McCloskey admitted he had difficulty distinguishing between a foul ball and a foul tip. But his son Dalton had a yen to play Little League Baseball. What then happened to Bill McCloskey of Williamsport and his son would be repeated many

"Mr. Baseball"—Connie Mack—was one of the first of many major league boosters of the sport.

times in towns across America in the years ahead.

McCloskey purchased all the baseball books he could find and learned all he could about the game. Night after night and weekend after weekend, he played catch with his son Dalton. They literally learned the game of baseball together.

Dalton became a Little Leaguer and Bill McCloskey became an involved parent. In his final year of eligibility Dalton was the leading hitter and the best pitcher in his league.

The early uniforms were flannel, leather belts held up baggy pants, and the boys wore ankle-high sneakers with rubber soles. Pictured here is the 1948 model.

The end of World War II spurred the growth of organized sports throughout America. The spread of suburbia plus the desire of Americans to forget the horrors of the war and get on with the games of peace particularly encouraged the development of Little League Baseball. Summertime for the children of the late 1940s and early 1950s became a ceremony of ice cream and sunshine and Little League Baseball.

In 1946 Ray Keyes returned to Williamsport after five years in the service. "Never in my wildest dreams did I envision what had happened with Little League," he says. "It was boom, boom—the thing just mushroomed. The program was unique. The children had the status of playing in an organized fashion, the benefit of being helped out by adult volunteers. It seemed like everyone wanted to be a part of it."

By 1946 Pennsylvania had a dozen leagues, the majority of them in Williamsport. The Brandon League of Williamsport was typical of the postwar programs.

"One thing I can't forget is the trouble we had getting uniforms," said Jack Sargent, who managed the Brandon League's first pennant-winner. "That was the first year after the war, and a lot of materials were hard to come by. But we were suited up by opening day. The uniforms were flannel; leather belts held up baggy pants. The boys wore ankle-high canvas sneakers with rubber soles. That's a far cry from the trim suits and low-cut shoes of today, but it was state of the art back then.

"The Brandon League was named for the city-owned park where we built a diamond," Sargent added. "The other leagues that originated in 1946 in Williamsport were named Lincoln and Sunday School."

As more leagues developed, baseball and district rivalries intensified. An incident that took place in 1947 characterized the poignancy that would always be part of children playing Little League Baseball.

A big playoff game was scheduled in Williamsport. Two boys, lifelong friends, were the oppos-

By 1947, when the Little League World Series began, there were sixty teams in two states. Here a player heads for home in a series game in the late 1940s.

ing pitchers in this game. They traveled to the big game on the same bicycle; one pedaled while the other perched on the bike's crossbar. Each was dressed in his team's uniform. When they got to the ballfield they parked the bike, wished each other well, and separated toward opposite dugouts.

The game began and moved on. Inning after inning each pitcher took his turn on the mound, holding the opposition scoreless. It was a nail-biting affair. The game moved into the final inning. Not a run had been scored by either side. Then the youth who owned the bicycle came to the plate to face his friend. Their eyes met for an instant. On a pitch that some said was out of the strike zone, the batter swung and hit a home run. The final score was 1-0.

The game concluded, the two youths left the field as they had arrived. The winning pitcher pedaled; the losing pitcher sat on the crossbar, tears streaming down his cheeks.

There were sixty teams in fifteen leagues in two states by 1947, when the Little League World Series began. The first league outside of Pennsylvania had been formed in Hammontown, New Jersey. The Little League Baseball dream was on the march.

The program's originators were overwhelmed by requests for information about how to start new leagues and directions on how to manage teams. What had begun as a neighborhood effort to give boys an organized baseball experience was turning into a movement involving close to a thousand children and their supporting adult cast, and the numbers were growing every year.

At about this time Carl Stotz became concerned that the steel-spiked shoes normally worn by ballplayers posed safety problems. He wondered whether a canvas-top shoe with rubber cleats could be developed as a special shoe for Little Leaguers.

Stotz contacted various corporations, including the United States Rubber Company, which had a factory in Williamsport. He was invited to meet with company officials in New York City. As a result United States Rubber was granted "exclusive" rights to manufacture the Little League shoe, although its board of directors decided for purposes of general good will to allow any firm to make them as long as strict specifications were met.

Linkage with the giant corporation proved a godsend for Little League Baseball. Not only was a safety concern addressed with the manufacture of the shoe, but the United States Rubber company agreed to become a national sponsor of Little League as well.

"Things became much more organized once the company got involved," noted Putsee Vanucci, a Williamsport photographer who began taking Little League pictures with his 4-by-5 Speed Graphic in 1940. "You could see with U.S. Rubber there the program would have to grow, that it would no longer be a hit-or-miss thing. They were pros, real marketing people."

In 1948 the United States Rubber Company underwrote the entire World Series tournament, paid for the transportation of out-of-town teams, furnished hotel accommodations, and gave out awards. In 1949 the company assumed all expenses for a national headquarters and paid Carl Stotz a salary as full-time commissioner of Little League Baseball. John Lindemuth was named assistant to the commissioner.

The combination of the United States Rubber Company acting as a kind of financial angel and an army of volunteers who so willingly gave of their time and energy enabled Little League Baseball to continue to expand. As the 1940s came to an end, Little League Baseball fields were sprouting all over the United States. In some areas, there were difficulties in locating suitable sites. However, even these hurdles were surmounted by the enthusiastic and growing cadre of volunteers willing to pitch in.

In Naugatuck, Connecticut, many options for a field were debated and discussed before sponsors paid for excavation work that burrowed out the side of a hill. More than 3000 cubic yards

In 1948 the United States Rubber Company underwrote the entire World Series tournament, paid for the transportation of the out-of-town teams, furnished hotel accomodations, and gave out awards.

By 1949 there were 867 teams in 197 leagues spread over a dozen states. Here a winning team from that year heads for the dugout.

of earth were dug and used to lay out a playing field. Frank "Spec" Shea, a Naugatuck resident and former New York Yankees pitcher, donated trucks from his firm so that the earth could be moved to create the field. Grateful citizens named the completed diamond the Peter J. Foley Field in honor of Shea's high school coach.

The tiny village of Sherwood, Ohio, had a similar problem. The only available playing site was split by a ravine. Hundreds of people from the little community went to work. Digging out and carting away massive amounts of earth, local residents built a 24-foot conduit, filled in the gully, and created a Little League playing field. But still another problem challenged the folks in Sherwood. In that farming community the need for youngsters to perform numerous daytime chores made it impossible for them to play Little League Baseball. Community members pitched in to set up a lighting system for night baseball.

Waverly, New York, also grappled with the problem of establishing a Little League field. However, there the requirement was one of bringing in landfill rather than taking it out. Volunteers trucked in fifteen hundred loads of earth, using twenty-four trucks a day. And they got the job done: there was a brand-new Little League field for the boys of Waverly.

By 1949 there were 867 teams in nearly 197 leagues spread over a dozen states. With so much growth and so many different individuals involved in the program, the organizers felt there was a need for a permanent structure to monitor operations. As a result, in 1950 a nonprofit corporation known as Little League Baseball, Inc. was formed, with a charter and by-laws "to protect Little League from any chance of departure from its ideals and from any thought of commercialization." A board of directors was named to uphold and determine that purpose. By the time of Little League's incorporation in the state of New York 150,000 boys were playing in the program on 3333 teams in 770 leagues. In a dozen years of existence, Little League had spread to virtually every state in the union.

The early and difficult days of Little League—when Carl Stotz had to cajole merchants to become sponsors of teams and leagues—were a thing of the past. In Miami, as soon as Little League was introduced forty-one sponsors competed for the four spots then open. A league in Miami Beach was wholly sponsored by the police and fire departments.

In 1952 a team from Montreal became the first foreign entry in the Little League World Series, just one year after Canada chartered the first Little League program outside the U.S. borders. The program was beginning to become international.

In the early 1950s, at the invitation of the United States government Stotz and Lindemuth visited Germany, France, England, and Morocco. "The government felt that American boys living in those countries, the children of armed forces personnel, should have the opportunity to play Little League Baseball, just like the kids in the United States," Lindemuth recalled. "At first it was just the American kids on the military bases. Gradually native children joined in."

In the Far East, a different situation developed. When Little League Baseball arrived in South Korea in 1951 it was a sad and war-ravaged nation. A native of Tucson, Arizona, U.S. Army chaplain Paul C. Hutchins had

The team from Montreal, Quebec, was the first foreign entry in the Little League World Series, in 1952.

been involved in Little League Baseball through his son. Deeply affected by the plight of Korean boys, observing the toll the war was taking on their personalities, Hutchins determined to bring some of the innocence and pleasures of youth into their lives. Through his efforts the Arizona Little League agreed to sponsor a Korean league. They sent baseballs and other equipment. Korean Little League began to take root.

Through the long, humid summer Korean boys who had never played baseball were tutored by American GIs. Two units of the Korean base section—the 335th Ordnance Ammunition Battalion and the 167th Transportation Truck Battalion—provided coaches, managers, trainers, and umpires.

While jet planes flew overhead and tanks and trucks headed for the battlefield, a makeshift version of Little League Baseball went on. The exigencies of war made playing schedules flexible. Stones and rocks had to be removed to create playing surfaces. There were no grassy infields or cutout diamonds and balls took bad hops, sometimes bruising the bodies of the new Little Leaguers.

Many of the Korean boys had never before worn a pair of shoes. Many of them were barely three feet tall and weighed no more than eighty pounds. Many had personally witnessed the horrors of the war—burning villages, death and destruction. In this horrendous environment Little League Baseball was like a wind of normalcy. And the Korean youth took to the game of baseball just like their American counterparts.

"We knew we were doing something wonderful for the kids," one GI recalled. "It didn't matter who won or who lost the games. What Little League Baseball did was to help those Korean boys forget for a time the war and the death. It was also a good thing for all of us GIs. We sort of adopted those Korean kids. We loved them, and they loved us."

What had begun as an inspired and altruistic gesture by an army chaplain helping out sad and forlorn youth would one day result in something no one in 1951 could ever anticipate: Korea becoming a powerhouse in the world of Little League Baseball.

After the Korean conflict came to an end in 1953 and the American GIs went home, Little League Baseball remained. The program would spread to other nations in the Far East, where it not only became a game for children to play but also a vehicle that would cross international boundaries, assuage suspicions and hostilities, and help to heal old wounds.

"As most people know," observed Dr. Creighton J. Hale, current president and CEO of Little League, "Korea and Japan have not exactly been friendly toward each other since Japan's occupation of Korea during World War II. Despite that lingering animosity thousands of Little League volunteers from both nations have been working together on behalf of the program for years."

Hale recalled an incident that took place with Guam district administrator Greg Calvo. "Taken captive by the Japanese during World War II and physically brutalized, all he could think about was getting revenge. Some years after the war, Calvo was the manager of the winning Little League team on Guam. Its next level of play was in Tokyo. Calvo, apprehensive over visiting Japan because of his intense feelings, decided nevertheless to go—because of the kids.

ABOVE: *The entry of teams from the Far East had a dramatic impact on the face of Little League.* RIGHT: *This photo of Dr. Creighton Hale with Little Leaguers clearly shows Little League's international scope.*

"Calvo told me," Hale said, "that seeing the innocent faces of the Japanese boys, he realized for the first time that there was a big difference between the Japanese military and the Japanese people. It was a big turning point in his life. Today he regularly visits Japan and frequently receives Japanese guests into his home in Guam. He readily admits that all of this never might have happened were it not for Little League Baseball."

And had it not been for Dr. Herman Goldberg, Little League Baseball would probably not have been planted in Italy. As it was, the good doctor had a bit of a struggle. Goldberg was superintendent of schools in Rochester, New York, and a coach in the Cobb's Hill Little League during the 1950s. Awarded a Fulbright fellowship, Goldberg took a leave of absence to pursue research and study in Italy.

A zealot as far as Little League Baseball was concerned, the Rochester educator set to work on getting the Italians to develop a program. Back home, Goldberg was accustomed to delegating authority as a school superintendent. He made having his instructions carried out with great precision a habit. However, giving directions in Italy, Dr. Goldberg would discover, would prove a different matter than in Rochester.

Goldberg painstakingly specified the dimensions and requirements for a Little League playing field. "You'll have to cut out grass to create base paths and batters' boxes," he pointed out.

"But, Dr. Goldberg," the Italian workers protested, "here in Italy, in this section, the grass has grown for centuries. It is beautiful. How can we cut it out? How can we destroy it?"

"You aren't destroying," the educator replied. "You are creating a playing field. This is what must be done."

Time passed. Goldberg returned to the rigors of his Fulbright study. One day he came back to survey the status of the Little League field under construction. He was pleased to note that all was in good order except for one puzzling thing: no grass had been cut out for the left-handed batter's box.

"Why hasn't the grass been cut out here?" he asked.

"Too much grass has been taken away already," Goldberg was told. "We don't need any more cutting."

"But what about the left-handed batters?"

"Dr. Goldberg, we haven't got that many left-handers. And those that are can bat off the grass."

The story goes that the grass in the left-handed batter's box was

Peter J. McGovern, who had been director of public relations for U.S. Rubber in Detroit, joined Little League on a "temporary loan" basis and ended up staying thirty-one years.

ultimately removed, but it took all of Dr. Goldberg's persuasive powers to get the job done properly.

Soon after the United States Rubber Company became involved with Little League Baseball, its officials realized someone was needed to help organize and coordinate the rapidly developing program. Peter J. McGovern, who had been the director of public relations for U.S. Rubber in Detroit, joined Little League on a "temporary loan basis" and ended up staying for thirty-one years.

"Mr. McGovern was a big man, a former great athlete, an oarsman who had been on teams that had established world records at the University of Pennsylvania," said Beverly Gray, who began with Little League in 1951 and became McGovern's secretary in 1956. "He was a true gentleman in every sense of the word," said Gray, who would become corporate secretary in 1969. "I was with Mr. McGovern right from the beginning."

From the beginning, however, there were ideological and philo-

New Jersey
CHAMPIONS
3

In a timeless scene, the New Jersey championship team honors the star of a winning game in the 1952 World Series.

sophical differences between McGovern and Carl Stotz that would never be resolved and would ultimately result in Stotz leaving the program.

McGovern became Little League Baseball president in 1952, a position he would retain for the next twenty-one years, and chairman of the board of directors in 1955—staying on in that capacity until his retirement in 1983. Under his direction Little League Baseball experienced its most phenomenal growth.

By 1953, the year the first *Little League Magazine* was published, there were 2800 leagues spread over forty-eight states. The children of Alaska and Hawaii played Little League Baseball before those areas had statehood. Puerto Rico, Canada, the Panama Canal Zone, the Dutch East Indies, and the Philippines had Little League Baseball programs by the mid-1950s.

Wherever there was Little League there was always a human-interest story reported in the press that unfailingly charmed the public. In Houston, Texas, for example, Little League Baseball was being established in the mid-1950s. Three sponsors signed up immediately; but there was a bit of a problem locating the fourth and final sponsor. Then someone thought of Eddie Dyer, who owned an insurance agency and was a leading resident of Houston in the off season. At that time Dyer was also the manager of the St. Louis Cardinals.

"Count me in, partner," drawled Dyer. "I'm willing."

Jeff Cross, one-time Cardinal infielder, volunteered to manage the Dyer-sponsored team, so the kids on that Houston squad even picked up some professional tutoring. When the Cardinals stopped in Houston on their way north from spring training, some of the team's biggest stars (like Stan Musial) were on hand to give the kids some big league tips.

One of the characters on that Houston team was Armand Tello, a pitcher. Outspoken, flamboyant, the youth seemed to thrive on getting into pitching jams and then working his way out of them. Tello would load the bases with no outs and then settle back and retire the side. He would go to a 3-0 count on a bat-

ter and then rear back and strike the batter out. A common scene after those cliffhanging incidents was the sight of Tello's teammates swarming around him on the mound and pounding him on the back shouting "Attaway to go!"

In one game, however, Tello suffered a frustrating loss when his third baseman muffed a ball and made an error. Manager Cross rushed out onto the field to offer solace.

"You were great, Tello," said Cross, draping his arm around the youth's shoulder. "Don't feel badly."

Tello responded with a big smile. "I don't feel sad, Mr. Cross. These boys on the team"—the boy swept his hands about the playing field—"they idolize me."

The endearing quality of the Houston team was unfortunately not the total picture of Little League Baseball during the 1950s, however. Arnold White of St. Petersburg, Florida, who has been regional director since 1960 and whose affiliation with Little League goes back to 1951, recalled the acrimony and divisiveness of Little League Baseball in the South in 1955.

"Events that occurred that year," the soft-spoken Southerner recalled, "threatened to tear apart the program. One year earlier, leagues were organized in black communities in Charleston, South Carolina, and Pensacola, Florida. And, at that time, any league in its second year of existence could apply to enter tournament play. So in 1955 the black teams did. However, the man who was the leader of Little League Baseball in South Carolina back then was adamantly opposed to any competition between white and black teams.

"This man had so much influence that all the other fifty-five chartered leagues in South Carolina and many more in other Southern states withdrew from the Little League program. Many of them have never returned. The team from Charleston was left with no team to compete against.

"At the same time, a similar kind of thing happened in the panhandle section of Florida. Segregationist fervor led to a mass refusal on the part of white teams to play the black team from Pensacola. But I am proud to say the staff of Williamsport stepped in courageously. They did the right thing. Since the Pensacola team had no competition, the people at Williamsport ruled they be brought into our

Another run scores in a game from the 1952 Little League World Series.

Florida state tournament where they were matched up against an all-white team from Orlando.

"That time was probably the most difficult of all my thirty-eight years in Little League Baseball," White continued. "There was much debate and discussion, all kinds of controversy over whether a game between a white and black team should be allowed to be played in a city-owned park in Orlando. You have to remember that in the mid-1950s the segregation issue was very prominent in the minds of many people. This game became more than an item in the sports pages. There were headlines on the front pages and national newspaper coverage.

"While the debate raged, other cities throughout Florida and military bases that had leagues extended invitations to enable the game to be played. They told us if the Orlando City Commissioners turn us down and won't let us play, they will accommodate the tournament on their site and pay all the expenses of the two teams.

"But, happily, the City of Orlando decided to let the game be played," White said. "Moreover, they took steps to provide the manpower to make sure there would be no incidents. They did a remarkable job.

"When the game took place it was probably the first time in the history of the South that an all-black team in any sport played against an all-white team. Attendance at the park was overflowing. It was probably one of the largest crowds that ever watched a Little League Baseball game in Florida to that point in time. At the playing site all the whites sat in one section. Blacks were restricted to another area. The black team lost the game. But even back then we understood what was really important—that Little League Baseball had scored the most significant victory."

As for the team from Charleston that had no team to play against, its members were guests of Little League Baseball at the World Series that August. "That was the statement that Little League made during this difficult time," White said, "and it is that a child is a child regardless of race, religion, or ethnic background. That is the historic philosophy of Little League Base-

Bill Shea (standing with Ted Williams), the man for whom Shea Stadium is named, today heads the Little League Foundation.

ball. It's always been that way, and it always will be."

The year 1955 was also a kind of crossroads for Little League Baseball. All sorts of organizational innovations characterized the program that year.

The Little League Pledge was written by Peter J. McGovern and the Little League Foundation incorporated in 1955. As detailed in its charter, the foundation is "an agency established to insure Little League's future, protect its ideals and extend its benefits." Former postmaster general James A. Farley was its first president. Today William A. Shea, a prominent New York City attorney and the man for whom Shea Stadium is named, heads the foundation. Other current members include William T. Cahill, former governor of New Jersey and the man instrumental in getting Congress to grant a charter to Little League Baseball; Jack Kent Cooke, owner of various sports franchises; Abraham Feinberg, New York City businessman; Joseph P. Flannery, executive of Uniroyal—the current name of the enterprise that was once U.S. Rubber; Eric M. Hilton, head of Hilton International; Bob Hope, show-business personality; Robert Kloss, executive vice president of the Presbyterian Minister's Fund, who also manages the finances for the Foundation; Dennis Lewin, senior vice president/production, ABC-TV Sports; G. Herbert McCracken, famed University of Pittsburgh athletic personality; Tatsuzo Mizukami, former chairman of the board and today senior adviser to the Mitsui Corporation; Peter

1955 (the year of this photo) saw many innovations, including the incorporation of the Little League Foundation and the origin of the Little League pledge.

O'Malley, owner of the Los Angeles Dodgers; V. J. Skutt, head of Mutual of Omaha Life Insurance; Alfred J. Stokely, Indianapolis businessman.

The sixteenth year of Little League's existence also saw the introduction of elected district administrators. Five men from the ranks of district administrators were elected to serve on Little League's Board of Directors. State directors were appointed. An apparatus for an annual meeting was created, and the first Little League Congress was held in Chicago in 1956.

What had begun as a loosely organized baseball program for youth was still geared to its original purpose, but now a tighter, more organized institutional framework was in place. In that crossroads year of 1955 Peter J. McGovern assumed the additional responsibilities of chairman of the board of directors of Little League Baseball, and an additional figure who would loom large in the organization's future joined the staff. Dr. Creighton J. Hale, then an associate professor of physiology at Springfield College in Springfield, Massachusetts, took a leave of absence to, in his words,

The radial-rib batting helmet developed by Dr. Creighton Hale was put into use in 1959. Here it is seen on a player sliding into home plate.

"conduct research on the effects of competition on young players." At that time there was much concern that competition had an adverse effect on youngsters. "My findings and those of other researchers contradicted that theory," Hale said. "In fact, it is now generally believed that competition is beneficial."

Hale had always been interested in athletics and still recalls his days "playing a lot of ball in the fields on the farm where we lived in Hardy, Nebraska. I was a twelve-letter sports winner in high school, and people referred to me as 'Hale and Hardy'—without realizing Hardy was where I came from."

Hale would prove to be an interesting counterpoint to McGovern, whose management skills were adding so much to the Little League program. With Hale on the scene, Little League Baseball was to become a leader in the development of safety innovations for youth.

Beverly Gray remembered when Hale came to Little League from Springfield: "He came just to do some research. But Little League was so impressed with him, they wouldn't let him go. He was enormously attracted to the program, and, from the start, he was a tremendous asset."

"I don't know how Creighton has done it," added Ray Keyes. "I'd come to work at six in the morning and see him there at the

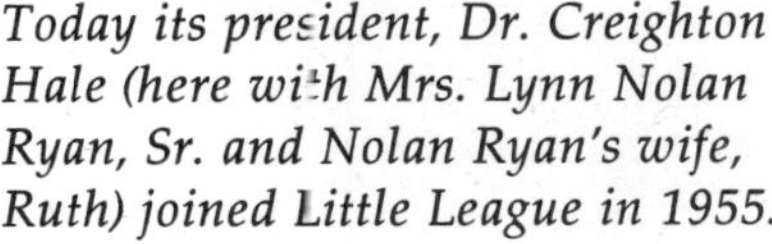

Today its president, Dr. Creighton Hale (here with Mrs. Lynn Nolan Ryan, Sr. and Nolan Ryan's wife, Ruth) joined Little League in 1955.

post office getting the mail. It was that way when he first started. It's still that way. He's always on the go for Little League."

Many of the safety innovations used today throughout baseball were developed for Little League Baseball by Creighton Hale. In the late 1950s, there was concern that Little League batters were hit by more fast balls than major league batters were. Hale experimented by wiring the throwing fingers of pitchers to an electric clock. "We timed the flight of the ball from the pitcher's fingertips to home plate," he said. "We calculated the speed of the pitch and the reaction time of the batter in both Little League and the major leagues."

Using mathematical ratios, it was determined that the Little League pitcher's mound was too close. As an added margin of safety the Little League mound was moved back two feet. All across America five thousand pitching mounds were dug up within the space of a year. Hale is still amazed at how cooperative the Little League volunteer community was. "They dug up the mounds," he said; "no debate, no argument. It was a testament to how sensitive the people in our program are to the safety needs of youth."

Player safety has been an ongoing concern of Little League. Metal spikes for shoes are not allowed. Night play is limited. Strict limitations exist on the use of pitchers.

The padded, double-earflap batting helmet developed by Hale for Little League has become a standard in all of amateur baseball and at some professional levels.

Joint research with Alcoa developed the aluminum bat that has made the wooden bat virtually obsolete in amateur baseball. "Previous aluminum bats," Hale pointed out, "were never functional because they would dent. Although the aluminum bat costs more initially, because it is unbreakable it saves leagues and school systems a good deal of money. And it does not splinter as does a wooden bat."

Under Hale's supervision the catcher's chest protector was also modified to provide better pro-

A Little Leaguer learns how to hold a bat, one of the aluminum type that has made the wooden bat virtually obsolete in amateur baseball.

LOUISVILLE SLUGGER
CHAMPIONS

tection for the throat, shoulder, and groin. First tested in the mid-1960s by Johnny Bench of the Cincinnati Reds, the modified chest protector is now mandatory in Little League and used by most professional catchers. Another safety-equipment innovation pioneered by Hale and Little League Baseball is the catcher's helmet with an attached mask.

In 1959, the year the radial-rib batting helmet developed by Hale was put into use, a presidential proclamation by Dwight D. Eisenhower designated the week beginning the second Monday in June as National Little League Baseball Week throughout the United States. Five years later, in July 1964, Little League Baseball was granted a federal charter under Public Law 88-378, which was signed by President Lyndon B. Johnson. "When the Congress of the United States incorporated Little League federally," Hale said, "it placed the program alongside the Boy Scouts of America and the American Red Cross." Little League Baseball thus became the only sports organization to be granted a charter of incorporation by the United States government. "That showed how far the program had come," Hale observed. The granting of a charter of incorporation by the United States government to Little League was the highest honor the federal government could bestow on the program.

During the tumultuous 1960s, a time of social unrest, changing mores and values, and war, Little League Baseball received the highest honor human beings could provide. Combat soldiers in Vietnam, many of whom had been Little Leaguers, adopted and supported teams back home.

An especially poignant linkage was between the Fourth Battalion "Spearheaders" and a team located 5000 miles away—the Senior White Sox of the Westbury American Little League of Houston, Texas. American soldiers who made up part of the Riverine Force patrolling the dangerous Mekong Delta in South Vietnam sent money to sponsor the White Sox team. "Our doing that," one of the soldiers said, "reminds us of all the good things in life—home, peace, freedom, playing baseball. . . . "

Little League proved a constant during a decade scarred by bitter divisiveness. Aided by its army of volunteers, the program expanded its reach and its scope.

In 1961, Senior League Baseball was originated for players thirteen to fifteen years old to give teenagers an opportunity to begin or continue their Little League experience. Today it is the world's largest program for that age group, with over 3500 leagues. Senior League Baseball is played on a conventional ninety-foot diamond and has a full range of tournament play, with a World Series staged every year at Kissimmee, Florida.

In 1962, the Little League Summer Camp was inaugurated in Williamsport and other cities with 245 campers. The following year ABC-TV televised the Little League championship game of the World Series to nations all over the globe.

The classic wooden "Louisville Slugger" bat shown here is rarely used today. Its tendency to splinter led to its replacement by the aluminun bat.

ABC's "Wide World of Sports" was not quite two years old when ABC executive Roone Arledge approached Little League officials offering to televise the World Series title game. On August 24, 1963, the first ABC transmission of a championship game took place. The original telecasts were taped and shown a week later, then ABC began taping the title game at 2:00 P.M. EST and broadcasting it three hours later the same day. Since 1985 telecasts have been live. ABC play-by-play announcers assigned to Little League World Series games include some legendary names—Mel Allen, Red Barber, Jim McKay, Keith Jackson, Al Michaels, Chris Schenkel, and Curt Gowdy. Color commentators have included Mickey Mantle, Brooks Robinson, Johnny Bench, Carlton Fisk, Steve Stone, Davey Lopes, Don Drysdale, Joe Morgan, Don Sutton, Willie Stargell, and Earl Weaver.

In 1987 Jim Palmer, a former Little Leaguer and three-time Cy Young Award winner, provided the analysis for ABC-TV's twenty-fifth anniversary coverage of the Little League World Series on "Wide World of Sports."

In 1987, ABC-TV celebrated its twenty-fifth anniversary of LLWS coverage on "Wide World of Sports." On hand for Little League coverage that year were former Little Leaguer Al Trautwig calling the play-by-play, with former Little Leaguer and three-time Cy Young Award winner Jim Palmer providing the analysis. They were joined by Olympic basketball star Cheryl Miller doing feature interviews. The ABC-TV Little League World Series linkage is the second-longest-running event on "Wide World of Sports."

The silver anniversary of Little League Baseball was celebrated in 1964. The program by then encompassed 6546 charters in the Little League and Senior League divisions. That silver anniversary year also saw the debut of the Umpire Training School at Williamsport.

The Umpire Training School was the idea of Howard G. Gair, a man who was on the Little League scene from its beginnings in 1939 until a few days before his death in 1973 at the age seventy-eight. Gair was the home-plate umpire in the very first Little League game and for every World Series from 1947 to 1960. Adviser, innovator, confidant, Gair functioned as chairman for the rules committee and trainer of volunteer umpires. As a result of his training experiences, Gair envisioned what became the Umpire Training School. At the start, sessions run by Gair and

Peter McGovern talks with Howard Gair (RIGHT)*, who founded the Umpire Training School, and Frank Rizzo, who along with Gair, taught its first sessions for free.*

Frank Rizzo were free. Today a nominal fifty-dollars-a-week charge covers training, room, and board.

The volunteers in attendance acquire theoretical knowledge and actual experience through umpiring games played by Little Leaguers and Seniors in the summer camp program. The school has become so popular that many district administrators cover the cost of umpires attending, according to Frank Rizzo, who succeeded Gair as director of the program and currently functions as umpire consultant at Little League Baseball headquarters. "The value gained from attending the school," Rizzo said, "comes from arbiters returning to their leagues and passing on

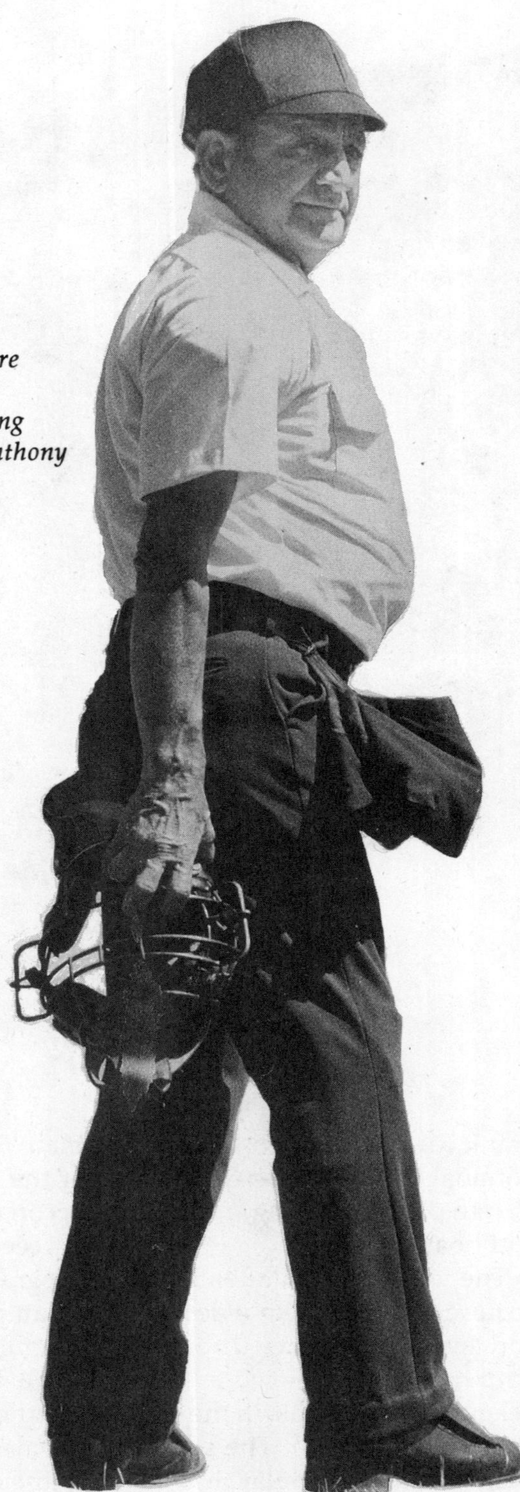

Frank Rizzo, currently an umpire consultant at Little League headquarters, began his umpiring career in 1941 when his son Anthony joined Little League.

their knowledge of rules and positioning to other umpires. Every state, plus Canada, Puerto Rico, and even Japan has sent participants to the umpire's school throughout the years."

Rizzo began his umpiring career in 1941 when his son Anthony joined Little League: "My boy was eight and played in the league, and they needed someone to umpire. I've been on the scene ever since." A founder of the Newberry League, one of the oldest still in existence, the gregarious septuagenarian who easily looks two decades younger readily admits "I've seen it all. We've had all kinds of people who have been attracted to the umpire's school. One for the books was Dr. Karl Way, who retired after forty-six years as an M.D. and began a new line of work. He came up to the umpire's school in Williamsport from Grove City, Ohio, and learned the 'tricks of the trade' pretty quickly. What he learned must have taken because into his eighties he was still making a twenty-two-mile trip on his motorcycle from his home to handle his umpiring duties. That's what I call dedication!"

Perhaps the most heroic example of a Little League umpire's dedication is that of Stanley David Koska. In 1986 Koska was umpiring a game in the Farrell Wheatland Little League in Farrell, Pennsylvania. A devastating tornado approached. Warning everyone to take cover, the thirty-six-year-old Koska huddled over two children in a ditch to protect them. Powerful winds ripped him from the children and flung him against a wall. Koska died. The children survived. Married for only a month at the time of his death, Koska had been a Little League umpire for six years.

The outstanding example of courage demonstrated by Stanley David Koska is part of the fabric of the Little League tapestry. Dr. Hale articulated his conception of the program's purpose: "Little League is not a baseball program, it's a leadership program. Our goals are to develop sportsmanship, teamwork, a desire to excel, international goodwill. We want to give an enjoyable, competitive experience to youngsters.

"Certainly the majority of major league baseball players come out of Little League today," Hale said, "but there are two and a half million youngsters playing Little League Baseball. Only a few hundred are playing major league baseball."

While Little League Baseball was never intended as a farm system for organized professional baseball, in effect it has become just that.

"Little League Baseball is the best farm system baseball has for development," noted former

One of Little League's army of dedicated volunteer umpires sweeps home plate in preparation for the next batter.

Baseball Commissioner Peter Ueberroth. "Kids who play Little League usually develop a lifelong affection for baseball and that is evident in major league baseball stadiums around the country." By the 1970s, as the baby boomers were coming of age, major league rosters were studded with stars who had once been Little Leaguers. In 1971 there was a total of forty-nine Little League Baseball graduates on Baltimore, Oakland, Pittsburgh, and San Francisco—the teams in the championship playoffs. In the World Series that year all of the Pittsburgh victories were recorded by pitchers Steve Blass, Bruce Kison, and Nelson Briles—three of the dozen Little League graduates on the Pirates World Championship roster.

By 1978 there were more than 2500 former Little Leaguers active in organized baseball. More than 300 played in the major leagues. In the 1978 major league All Star Game, thirty-two players were Little League Baseball graduates. Three players on the Belmont Heights team of Tampa, Florida, who competed in the 1979 Senior League World

Series in Gary, Indiana, were coveted by major league teams. Pitcher Vance Lovelace was a first-round choice of the Chicago Cubs in the 1981 draft. Dwight Gooden (who would go on to pitch for the New York Mets) and Floyd Youmans (who would be a hurler for the Montreal Expos) were the first-and second-round selections in the 1982 draft.

Although many youngsters have graduated from the ranks of Little League Baseball to the major leagues, only a handful have made it from foreign Little League teams to the majors. Two of these are Rick Mahler and Glenn Hubbard, who wound up for a time as teammates on the Atlanta Braves.

Mahler played his first three years of Little League Baseball at the High Wycombe Air Force Base outside London. "My father was in the Air Force and was our team's coach. They had a regular Little League team on the base," he recalled. "There were six teams just from the servicemen's families."

Hubbard had the unusual experience of playing for two years in Taiwan on the air force base. "My dad was in the Air Force for twenty years and was my first coach. We played our All Star teams against the best Taiwanese clubs. They were a powerhouse. When they went to the World Series in Williamsport, they were the best Little League Baseball team in the whole world."

By 1983 it was clear that Little League's major league "alumni association" boasted most of the best professional players in the world. The top vote-getters for major league baseball's All Star teams in all but three years since 1970 were former Little Leaguers. That elite list included top vote-getter Rod Carew plus Steve Garvey, Carlton Fisk, Mike Schmidt, Dave Concepcion, and George Brett. In the 1983 World Series there were eighteen former Little Leaguers on the ros-

By 1971, when this shot was taken, there was a total of forty-nine Little League graduates on teams in Baltimore, Oakland, Pittsburgh, and San Francisco—the teams in the championship playoffs.

ters of the Philadelphia Phillies and Baltimore Orioles.

Three years later Little League graduates won the Most Valuable Player awards in the American and National League Championship Series and the World Series. And the heroics of Gary Carter of the New York Mets and Marty Barrett of the Boston Red Sox highlighted the efforts of thirty-one former Little Leaguers in the fall classic.

The youngest American and National League Cy Young Award winners are both Little League graduates. Brett Saberhagen of the Kansas City Royals (who played in the Van Nuys Little League of Reseda, California) and Dwight Gooden of the New York Mets (a graduate of the Belmont Heights Little League of Tampa, Florida) both won their Cy Young Awards in 1986.

Jim Palmer (Beverly Hills, California, Little League); Tom Seaver (Spartan Little League of Fresno, California); Frank Viola (East Meadow, New York, Little League); Orel Hershiser (Atlantic Little League, Cherry Hill, New Jersey); Rollie Fingers (Cucamonga, California, Little League); and Steve Carlton (North Miami, Florida, Little League) are the others who share the distinction of being the only major leaguers and Little Leaguers to win the coveted award.

The relationship of Little

FROM LEFT TO RIGHT, *Gary Carter, George Brett, Steve Garvey, and Mike Schmidt are all Little Leaguers who have gone on to earn top honors in major league baseball.*

League Baseball to all major league teams is highly positive, but the organization that has perhaps the strongest relationship with Little League is the Los Angeles Dodgers.

"The late Walter O'Malley, back when he owned the Brooklyn Dodgers," reported Dr. Hale, "was a charter member of the Little League Foundation. He loved baseball and loved children. He was extremely devoted to our efforts.

"Peter O'Malley, like his father a member of the Little League Foundation, is also a good friend of Little League." Since 1976 the Los Angeles Dodgers have staged Little League nights. As a combination fund-raiser and night of fun for Little Leaguers, the Dodgers set aside thousands of tickets at half price and make them available to leagues for sale at a profit. "There has been so much interest in this program," Hale added,

New York Mets pitcher Dwight Gooden, who began his baseball career in the Belmont Heights Little League of Tampa (Fla.), won the Cy Young Award in 1986.

"that the Dodgers have had to set aside ten dates a year to accommodate the fifty thousand or more who want to attend."

A change of guard in the executive leadership of Little League Baseball took place in 1973. Peter J. McGovern, on the scene as president since 1952, stepped aside and was succeeded by Dr.

Creighton J. Hale. McGovern remained as chairman of the board of directors and chief executive officer. The new president immediately found himself and Little League Baseball in the front lines of a heated national controversy.

As a public institution dealing with children, Little League Baseball has always had to contend with and been affected by the winds of social and political change. In the early 1970s, the women's movement sought to have girls play Little League Baseball.

"It wasn't that anyone had anything against girls," said John Lindemuth. "It was just that throughout most of the years of the program the issue never came up. Discrimination of any kind has always been frowned on by Little League Baseball.

"Remember that when Little League first began a lot of activities in America were segregated," Lindemuth continued. "But Little League right off the bat was against any kind of discrimination. I recall in the early 1950s, there was a Little League official coach in Maryland who told me: 'These kids don't know the difference between white or black unless we tell them. And we don't tell them!' "

Despite the nondiscrimination policy that had been in place from Little League's inception, battle lines were drawn on the issue of girls playing in the program. Some communities were split down the middle. Rhetoric escalated. In New York City, the American Civil Liberties Union went to court on behalf of seven girls. In other states the National Organization for Women and private lawyers were brought into the battle.

The controversy finally ended on June 30, 1974, when Little League Baseball announced that because of the "changing social climate" girls would be allowed to play on its teams.

That year of 1974 girls made even more progress in the world of Little League. Softball was introduced for girls aged eight to twelve; a tee-ball program was inaugurated for six to eight-year-olds. Today there is Senior League Softball for ages thirteen to fifteen and Big League Softball for ages sixteen to eighteen. Utilizing a sixty-foot diamond and a

LEFT: *On June 30, 1974, Little League Baseball announced that because of "changing social climate" girls would be allowed to play on its teams.*

pitching distance of forty feet, Little League Softball today numbers over more than fifteen hundred leagues and has a full range of tournament play including a championship World Series.

The newest extension of the Little League program is Big League Softball. A full range of tournament play is engaged in with a championship World Series.

While the women's movement in the United States led to an expansion of Little League Baseball to a new group of players, the winds of political conflict on the international scene buffeted and even restricted the program's growth in other parts of the

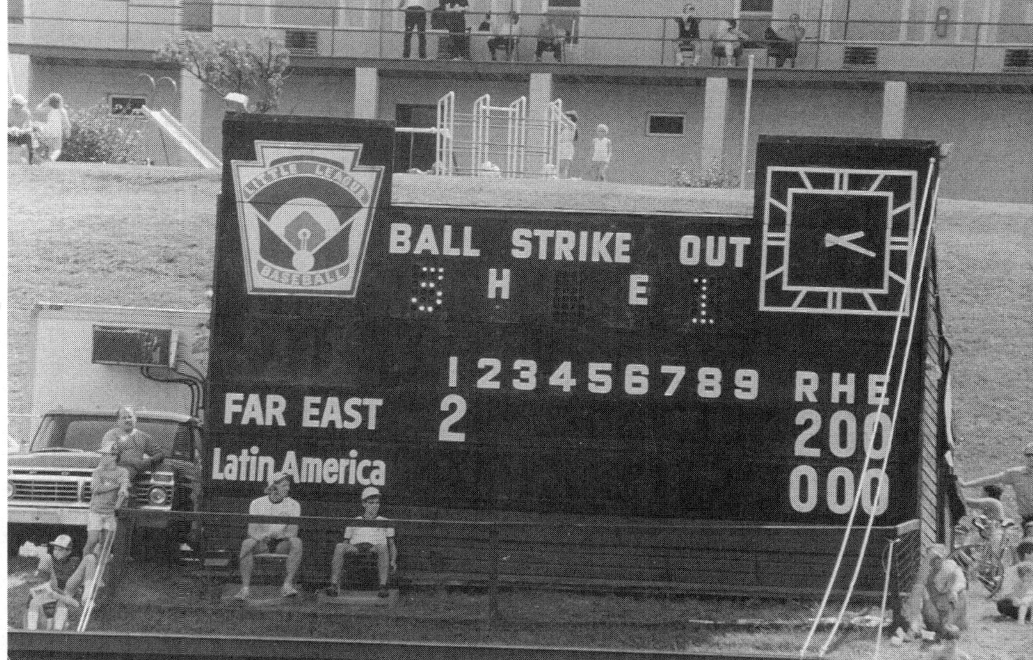

RIGHT: *Little League Baseball first went international in 1952. Today it is not unusual to see a World Series game contested by two teams from abroad.*

world during the 1970s and 1980s.

The Athens Little League was threatened with extinction when American military bases in Greece were in danger of being closed. That program, however, survives. El Salvador, which has maintained Little League charters since 1981, has had its programs threatened by the ongoing political strife in that nation. They too have survived.

Other nations have not fared so well.

Once there were Little League programs in Zimbabwe (formerly Rhodesia), South Africa, Ecuador, and Nicaragua. Political upheavals first curtailed and then finally ended Little League's existence in those countries. Libya and Iran had programs that became casualties of Middle East tensions and anti-American policies.

Despite these setbacks occasioned by forces beyond Little League's control, the program remains committed to prevailing and expanding on the international scene, to using Little League Baseball as a vehicle for the creation of international good will.

Joseph Losch, Little League's international tournament director, provided an example of the positive diplomacy Little League engenders. "Several years ago a team came to the series from inner-city Chicago," he recalled. "They were supposed to be rough, tough, streetwise kids, but when they got to Williamsport they turned out to be just the opposite. The only problem we had was consoling them when it was time for them to go home. They didn't want to leave the new friends they had made from other countries. And boy, did those Chicago kids bawl when they got on the bus for the airport. Today some of those Chicago kids remain pen pals of the kids they met from so many parts of the world—the Far East, Latin America, and Europe. And it's all due to Little League Baseball."

Those involved with Little League on the international level range through all levels of society just like their American counterparts. They run the gamut from average citizens to people like Tatsuzo Mizukami, who heads the Far East region. Little League Foundation member Mizukami is the former chairman of the board of the Mitsui Corporation of Japan, a company that does a multibillion dollar business a year. He recently donated $250,000 to build the first Little League Friendship Field in China, to allow for the program to develop in that country.

Although space is at a premium in or near Japanese cities,

Today Little League Baseball is played all over the world, soon even in the Soviet Union, China, and Israel. But, wherever it may be, it still comes down to kids playing their hearts out on a diamond.

that nation has nearly 400 Little League Baseball programs and ranks second to the United States in number of leagues.

The Jakarta (Indonesia) Little League was created in 1978 and is one of the more atypical international programs. While most of the overseas teams have historically been made up of children living at embassies or on military bases, Jakarta's Little League includes youth from Japan, Australia, Holland, and Germany in addition to kids from the United States. Despite the cultural and language barriers with such an international assortment in one league, the problems of playing baseball in an area of enervating humidity and high temperatures, and often tangled terrain bordered by lush jungles, the Jakarta Little League has thrived. Its enrollment doubled in the first year of its existence. By 1979 Jakarta's All Stars were competing in their first Far East Regional Tournament. One year later a second Jakarta Little League program had been created.

Panama had provided a good example of how Little League Baseball can expand in a politically stable situation. That small nation in 1984 had only ten programs but nevertheless managed to send a team from Panama City to represent the Latin American Region in the Little League World Series. A year later there were forty Little League programs in Panama.

Little League Baseball first went international in 1952, as we have seen. Dr. Hale, who succeeded Peer J. McGovern as chief executive officer in 1983, has been increasingly involved with promoting international Little League. He looks forward to an expansion and growth of programs abroad, particularly in light of the growing interest in baseball internationally and the fact that it will become a medal sport in the 1992 Summer Olympic Games in Barcelona.

"In countries where they have no baseball at all," noted Tim Hughes, vice president of operations, "Little League is the program of choice as a means of becoming competitive in a short time. European teams composed of youths who are dependents of U.S. military or diplomatic personnel are about to become a footnote to history. Now there will be native teams."

The growth of native teams comes from a realization that "to develop good baseball players a nation must start them off in their early years—their Little League years," as Dr. Hale has pointed out. Two native leagues are already chartered in Italy. Peru, Colombia, Finland, France, the Netherlands, Spain, Australia, and Israel are all gearing up to create Little League Baseball programs.

In Tokyo in June 1988, Hale and Peter O'Malley, owner of the Los Angeles Dodgers and a trustee of the Little League Foundation, announced plans for the development of the first Little League Friendship Field in China.

Little League Baseball in the Soviet Union as early as 1989 is a distinct possibility. "Developing international understanding and the qualities of teamwork, sportsmanship, and leadership will be the true value of Little League Baseball in the Soviet Union," Dr. Hale has said. "I'm optimistic that the good will that will result when Soviet Little Leaguers eventually play baseball against United States youngsters will be much like the sense of friendship developed when Japanese Little Leaguers first competed against United States kids following World War II."

With Little League Baseball "about to sprout up all over the Soviet Union, in China, Israel," Hale describes the present era as "a really exciting time."

In 1980 there were programs in thirty foreign countries and territorial possessions. "In a couple of years," Hale said, "there may be as many as fifty-five or sixty countries with Little League Baseball."

Another area where Little League Baseball will expand is in establishing programs for disabled Little Leaguers. It will be known as the Adaptive Play Division. "Once guidelines and training are developed for volunteers," promised Tim Hughes, "there will be Little League Baseball for exceptional children, children in wheelchairs, on crutches, with emotional and physical problems. All of them will be involved in what will become the newest division of Little League Baseball."

This aerial view shows the entire complex at Little League headquarters in Williamsport, Pennsylvania.

Expansion, education, innovation, excitement—all have been part of Little League's first fifty years and will be cornerstones of the program as it moves into its second half-century. The program that started as a three-team neighborhood league has been extolled in "Voice of America" programs as an example of American life.

What began with thirty boys in 1939 today involves more than two and half million participants spread over 7000 leagues worldwide. Regional centers exist throughout the United States: in Indianapolis, Indiana (central); St. Petersburg, Florida (southern); San Bernardino, California (western); Waco, Texas (Texas state headquarters); and Ottawa, Ontario (Canadian headquarters). A regional center is under development in Bristol, Connecticut.

But the center of Little League Baseball remains in the Pennsylvania town where it began. The Williamsport-based international headquarters has a forty-two-acre complex, a beautiful stadium, practice diamonds, living quarters for visiting teams, a recreation hall, and a junior Olympic-sized swimming pool.

Adjacent to the international complex on Route 15 in South Williamsport stands the the Peter J. McGovern Little League Baseball Museum. Opened on August 28, 1982, the $2.3-million colonial-style facility is the repository of Little League archives and memorabilia and a "hands-on" sound-and-sight attraction for thousands of visitors every year. On August 13, 1986, the museum welcomed its hundred thousandth visitor.

One of the largest photographic murals in the world (15 feet high and 110 feet long) greets the visitor who enters the Little League museum. The shot was taken from the pitcher's mound looking into the stands just before the start of the 1982 World Series championship game. Standing before it, one gets the sense of what it is like to watch or play Little League Baseball.

Young visitors to the museum, however, are more likely to race down the stairs to the lower level where the "Play Ball Room" is located. There they can try their skills in batting and pitching

For a youngster who plays in the Little League World Series in the big stadium in Williamsport the experience must be one of the most thrilling of his or her lifetime.

cages and then see their efforts played back on videotape.

Eight spacious and well-designed theme rooms guide visitors through collections of letters, photographs, and memorabilia that showcase the early years of Little League, the World Series, and world champions in the older divisions.

The showcase room houses Little League treasures from some of today's major league stars, and audio-visual highlights of World Series play. The "Play It Safe Room" documents the development of safety equipment. In the "Around the World Room," the push of a button visually guides one via a fiberoptic map to trace the growth of Little League Baseball from a single league to today's 7000 leagues all over the world. Then there is the "Diamond Theater"—a modern auditorium that shows films to visitors several times a day. And on one wall of the museum are letters from every president of the United States since Little League began. Etched on silver plaques, these letters are

an expression of the enthusiasm Little League has engendered at the highest levels of public life throughout its fifty-year history.

In the heat of Texas and Florida, in the cold spring of Minnesota and North Dakota, in the sapping humidity of Louisiana, in the high altitude of Utah and Colorado, on inner-city playgrounds in Chicago and Detroit, and in the wealthy suburbs of Long Island and Connecticut, Little League Baseball continues to thrive and expand.

The program has prevailed over changing social styles, the challenges of other youth programs, political trends, debates over safety and competition, even zero population growth that "held expansion to a minimum for a while," according to Tim Hughes.

A family, a community, Little League Baseball has been around for so long now through its ceremonies of summer, its moments of friendly competition on the playing field, its installation breakfasts and graduation dinners, that many things seem to flow one into another.

There are John Lindemuth and Frank Rizzo, circa 1940, and the millions since then, still involved actively or in reverie:

"Hey, Johnny Lindemuth!"

"Hello,"

"How are you?

"I'm fine. I'm sorry, but you're. . . ?"

"Don't you recognize me, Johnny?"

"Not with the beard and all, I don't. Give me a hint, will you?"

"I was in Little League Baseball."

Ceremonies of August

From its start there has been something splendid about the Little League Baseball World Series: the best youngsters spiritedly competing against each other in games of baseball. Ceremonious yet spontaneous, democratic yet controlled, intense yet carefree, the World Series is one of the world's great sporting events—where the best battle for bragging rights against the best.

The Little League Baseball World Series is a sports and cultural phenomenon that has evolved and grown grander through the years, yet it remains true to its roots—youth versus youth playing baseball in the August sun in the last days before a new school year begins.

Only eleven teams were entered in tournament play in 1947 for the first World Series. Today 7000 teams from all around the globe quest for the world championship. Each chartered Little League Baseball program in the world is eligible to enter one team in tournament play. Teams consist of fourteen players, a manager, and a coach. No player may be younger than eleven years old or older than twelve. Pitching rules are modified during tournament play, enabling a hurler to go nine innings in a game.

The smile tells the whole story in this scene from the 1967 World Series.

The team from Monterrey (Mex.) waves its sombreros in farewell as it leaves Williamsport at the conclusion of World Series competition.

Approximately 12,250 games are played in only seven weeks to determine the eight regional champions who meet in late August in Williamsport. The eight finalists represent four United States regions (East, West, South, and Central) plus four foreign regions: Canada, Europe, Latin America, and the Far East.

Admission to the World Series has always been free. And hundreds of thousands have come to Williamsport throughout the years to see the games. Hours before game time, the spectators assemble, bringing their ample lunchbaskets, picnic jugs, blankets, and lawn chairs to sit in the sun and watch the eleven-to-twelve-year-olds play ball.

"It's Christmas in August," reports a Williamsport businessman in an apt reference to the festive atmosphere that turns the small valley city nestled between the mountains in central Pennsylvania into a meeting place for people from all over the world.

Series week transforms an American town into an international city. Bright banners welcoming the teams from foreign nations flutter in the breeze over store windows, across bridges, and high above the streets. Signs in stores announce *On parle francais ici* for the benefit of French-speaking visitors—and there are also messages in German, Spanish, Chinese. The banners mingle with the traditional decorations of World Series memorabilia, bunting, and photographs.

"The idea of playing in a foreign country is a dream come true for our children," said Oscar N. Olivas, president of one of the Mexican Little League programs. "Most of our kids never traveled more than seven or eight miles from their homes. They are from minimum-wage families, dirt-poor families. But the thrill of their being thousands of miles away from home and competing in the Little League World Series is something that can never be taken away from them."

When the bus bringing foreign teams to Williamsport arrives, "it's nearly midnight" Tim Hughes, Little League vice president of operations, noted. "There's subtle lighting on the stadium. The kids get out of the bus and run down to the field. We warn them of the hills in the terraced stadium. But they scamper down and run all over the stadium. They scoop out a handful of dirt from the

field. It's precious soil to them. It's a precious moment for them."

During World Series Week the hotels and motels within Williamsport and in a fifty-mile radius are booked solid. Many out-of-towners take pride in their personal record of having attended the World Series for a quarter century or more. These fans book accommodations for the following year as soon as the series they are attending is over.

Pin-trading, whiffleball games, laughter, camaraderie, making new friendships and renewing old acquaintances—all are part of the texture of World Series week.

One of the most impressive moments of the Little League World Series takes place in pregame ceremonies. The Little League pledge is recited in the

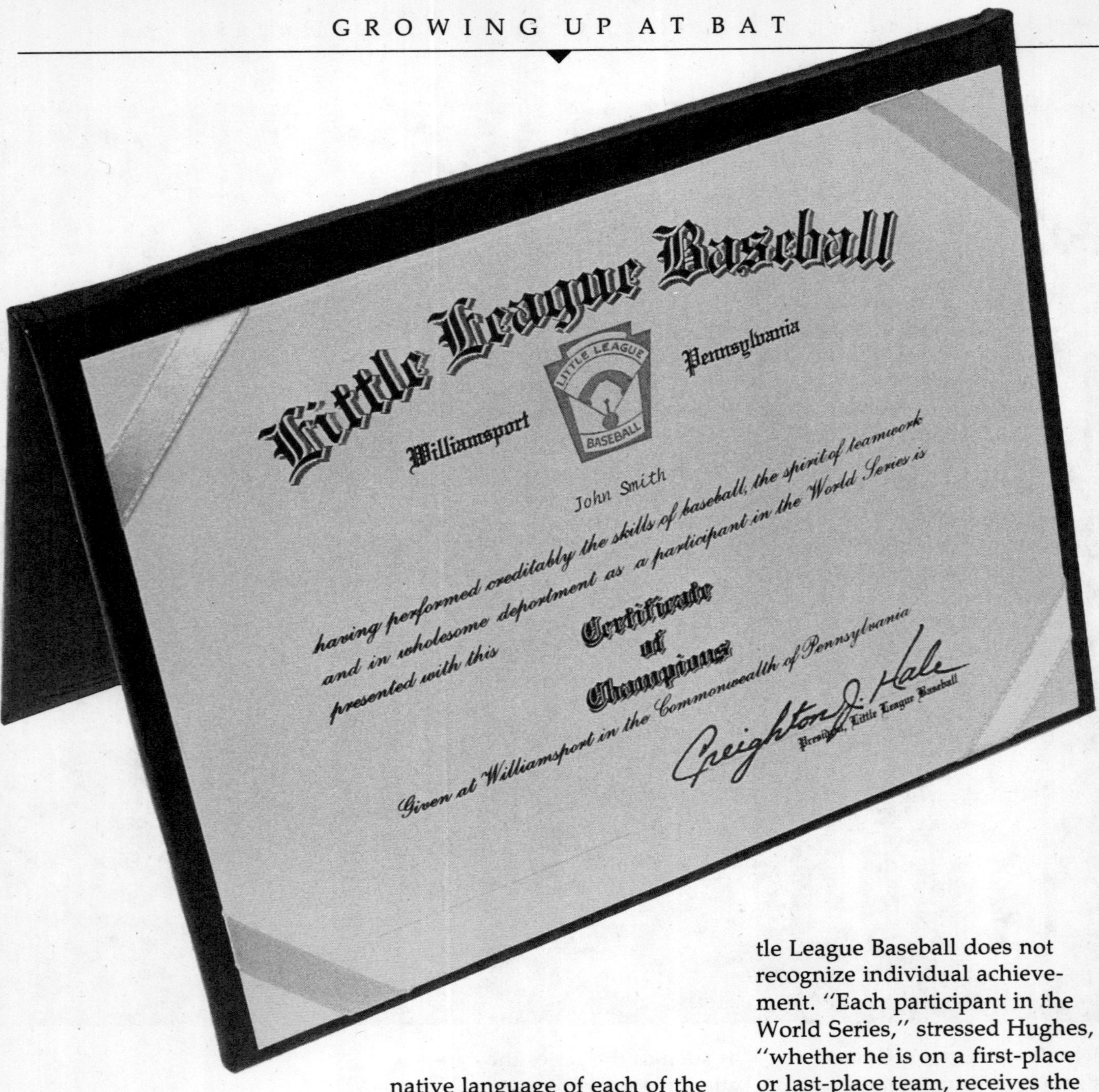

Each World Series participant recevies an eight-by-five certificate to signify that he or she took part in the World Series.

native language of each of the participating teams. The youth selected to cite the pledge in English holds a baseball cap over his heart and says: "I trust in God. I love my country and will respect its laws. I will play fair and strive to win, but win or lose, I will always do my best."

The World Series competition underscores the fact that Little League Baseball does not recognize individual achievement. "Each participant in the World Series," stressed Hughes, "whether he is on a first-place or last-place team, receives the same memento. It is a small pin, identical to what the youngster might've been awarded in the first game he ever played. The only difference is that the pin is a different color and says *World Series* on it."

"Little League Baseball's official position is conservative regarding all awards and certificates," Hughes added. "The

World Series participants receive an eight-by-five certificate that looks like a high school diploma. It simply signifies to all that they took part in the World Series."

On the local level Little League Baseball "does not encourage the giving of awards for individual achievement either," Hughes pointed out. "There is no recognition for the 'Best Pitcher of the Year' or for the kid who hits the most home runs. We allow recognition for team achievement for we recognize baseball as a team sport."

Through Little League Baseball's first fifty years, according to Hughes, objections to and criticisms of some of these policies have been raised. "But we have never wavered from them. And that is perhaps one of the singular aspects of the program that has kept it going, kept it expanding, kept it unique."

In 1947, the first World Series competition was called the National Little League Tournament. It was played at Memorial Park, nestled on a flat piece of land between a busy highway and a huge dike that protected the city of Williamsport from the spring floodwaters of the Susquehanna River. The setting was picturesque, a typical small-town park in America in the years following World War II. And although much has changed in the years since, the Williamsport Elks-Repaz Band still performs in the World Series today as it did in Memorial Park back in 1947.

Jack Losch was a member of the 1947 Maynard Midgets who competed against a team from Lock Haven in the championship game. "The Maynard League came about because we could not play in the original Little League since we were all living outside the established boundaries," Losch recalled. "The local Bethlehem Steel plant had donated land for the new Maynard League to play on. We were all excited to see the new field take shape: a lighted scoreboard, an outfield fence, base paths, real dugouts, a backstop, and a grass infield.

Each World Series participant, whether on a first-place or last-place team, also receives a small pin as a memento.

In 1947, in the first Little League World Series, the Maynard (Pa.) Midgets, shown here, defeated the team from the Lock Haven (Pa.) Little League.

Wow! It seemed as though we were living in a dream. The four league sponsors—Sears, Roebuck Company, Veterans of Foreign Wars, Forty and Eight Club, and Mossers Leather—provided all the kids on the teams with brand-new uniforms.

"The season started in June," Losch explained, "and we progressed through regular league play. Then we heard through the grapevine that there was going to be a national tournament and that they were going to pick an All-Star team to represent the Maynard League. It was great to be selected to play on that team and, although during the regular season I was a catcher, for the tournament play I was assigned to play the outfield and also be a back-up catcher.

"Each team in the Maynard League had representation on the All-Star team, and most of the kids were friends and schoolmates. We may have come from different ethnic, religious, and social backgrounds, but we felt the democratic spirit: we were a team

"Most of the teams were from around the local Williamsport area," Losch remembered, "because Little League was still in its infancy at that time. But there was one out-of-state entry—a team from Hammonton, New Jersey."

The Maynard Midgets and the Lock Haven Little League won their respective semi-final games to survive the competition in the field of eleven and meet in the championship game. "It was a natural rivalry," Losch said, "since our towns had matched up against each other in football and basketball for many years."

More than 2200 spectators came out on a muggy August afternoon to watch the action play out in Memorial Park. Hundreds took up nesting places on the grassy dike banks of Lycoming Creek behind the field. Others sat on cartops or watched the game from street-level positions.

"We never dreamed so many people would be interested in watching children play baseball," mused Howard Gair, who would be on the scene until 1959 as the World Series home-plate umpire. "The enthusiasm rubbed off on the youngsters," he said, "and the idea of a National Tournament that would become an annual event was firmly established."

The 1947 Maynard Midgets and the team from Lock Haven were uncomfortable in the summer heat in their wool uniforms, leftovers from the regular season. A few of the players were unsteady getting a footing in the batter's box in their ankle-high canvas sneakers.

"The game went back and forth, and we were all filled with butterflies," Losch recalled. "Every time Lock Haven got a hit, we were all pulling for our teammates to make the play. Every time one of us was at bat, we were all coaching him to get a hit. It was a total team effort. We wound up beating Lock Haven sixteen to seven."

Losch would go on to play football at the University of Miami and with the Green Bay Packers of the National Football League. Still, for him nothing would ever quite compare to the experience of that first Little League championship game: "I shall always remember that hot, humid August day, when a skinny little kid, covered with sweat and dirt and drained of strength by the elements, shared a magic moment with Don Stover, Frank Wool, Tony Ingersol, Butch Laurenson, Bill Gallagher, Lou Baity, Rusty Columbine, 'Buzz' Ungard, Ray Singley, Ed Jonas, Jim Sughrue, Walter Dunston, and Bob Smith . . . I can still remember each name."

In 1948, with the United States Rubber Company underwriting all costs of the World Series, the competition expanded to include teams from Vermont, Connecticut, and Florida. The 1947 second-place finisher, Lock Haven (Pa.) defeated St. Petersburg (Fla.) 6-5 in the title game before a crowd twice the size of the year before. And long after people forgot the score of that game they remembered a couple of colorful players who appeared in the '48 series.

Joe Cardamone, a stocky little catcher on Lock Haven, was

The Lock Haven (Pa.) team came back to the World Series in 1948 to win the championship over the team from St. Petersburg (Fla.).

The umpire makes a close call at home plate in the 1949 World Series.

one of them. Whenever an opposing player crossed the plate to score a run, the lively Cardamone would whip off his catcher's mask and vigorously shake the hand of the opponent. Another crowd-pleaser was Frank Rybczyk of Middletown (Ct.). His teammates called him Murphy; sportswriters smitten by his oversized pants called him "the uniform that walks like a boy."

In 1949, a World Series championship game was broadcast for the first time on radio. Ted Husing did the play-by-play as Hammonton (N.J.) shut out Pensacola (Fla.) 5-0. In that World Series one of the true phenomena of Little League Baseball emerged—a group of dedicated men affectionately called Uncles.

An "uncle" is a volunteer who hosts teams during World Series week in Williamsport. Tim Hughes commented on them: "They serve a tremendous function. There are two uncles for each team, making a total of sixteen uncles in all. They greet the team buses and escort the kids to their cabins. And they remain with the boys all week from sunup to beyond sundown."

All of the uncles are Williamsport residents. They plan their vacation time around World Series week. The total combined years of service of the uncles exceeds two hundred years.

W. Russ Swartz is the acknowledged dean of the uncles. On the job for over three decades now, Swartz recalled the early days of the World Series: "There was more community involvement than there is now. At first the kids stayed at a downtown hotel, then they moved on to Lycoming College. They ate at churches. The whole town got involved with the kids. We'd take them for boatrides on the Susquehanna River. We even had a day in the country for them. It made for more work for us, but we got more involved with the boys."

Howard R. Baldwin has been an uncle since 1950. "I can't sit by as an adult and complain about what kids might or might not do with their lives if I don't do something to help them," he said. "Little League is a means by which boys and girls mold their generation with that of their parents. But nothing is accomplished unless you find individuals who are willing to work with the children."

An uncle for more than three decades before his death, Gene F. Grambling maintained that his most memorable moment took place in a hospital room. "I was hosting a team from Pearl City, Hawaii, one year, and it was a pretty difficult time for me," he recalled. "My daughter Chris, who was just ten years old at the time, was sick in the hospital all during the World Series.

"But what a lift I got—and so did my daughter, of course—when the parents of the Hawaiian players showed up one evening at the hospital and gave Chris leis and pineapples. After the series I struck up a conversation with those people, and it continues today."

"Being an uncle is a coveted job," explained Tim Hughes. "There's an expression in Williamsport, 'once an uncle, always an uncle.' The position does not turn over very often."

The 1950 World Series saw

a team "from Texas managed by one-time St. Louis Cardinal infielder Joffre Cross pay its own way to get to Williamsport," according to John Lindemuth. "But they got as far as Harrisburg and then their money ran out. We got a call at five in the morning, and about a half-dozen of us drove down in our own cars and picked them up. We quartered the team in a Williamsport church and took good care of them all the time they were here."

Larry Fogarty, a center fielder on that Houston team, remembered "We were all in hog heaven. You're talking about a bunch of twelve-year-old boys who had never been out of Texas."

That Houston team would meet Bridgeport (Ct.) in what would prove to be a highly controversial championship game. Johnny Lewis, the only black player in the tournament,

The team from New York celebrates after winning a game in the preliminary rounds in the 1950 World Series.

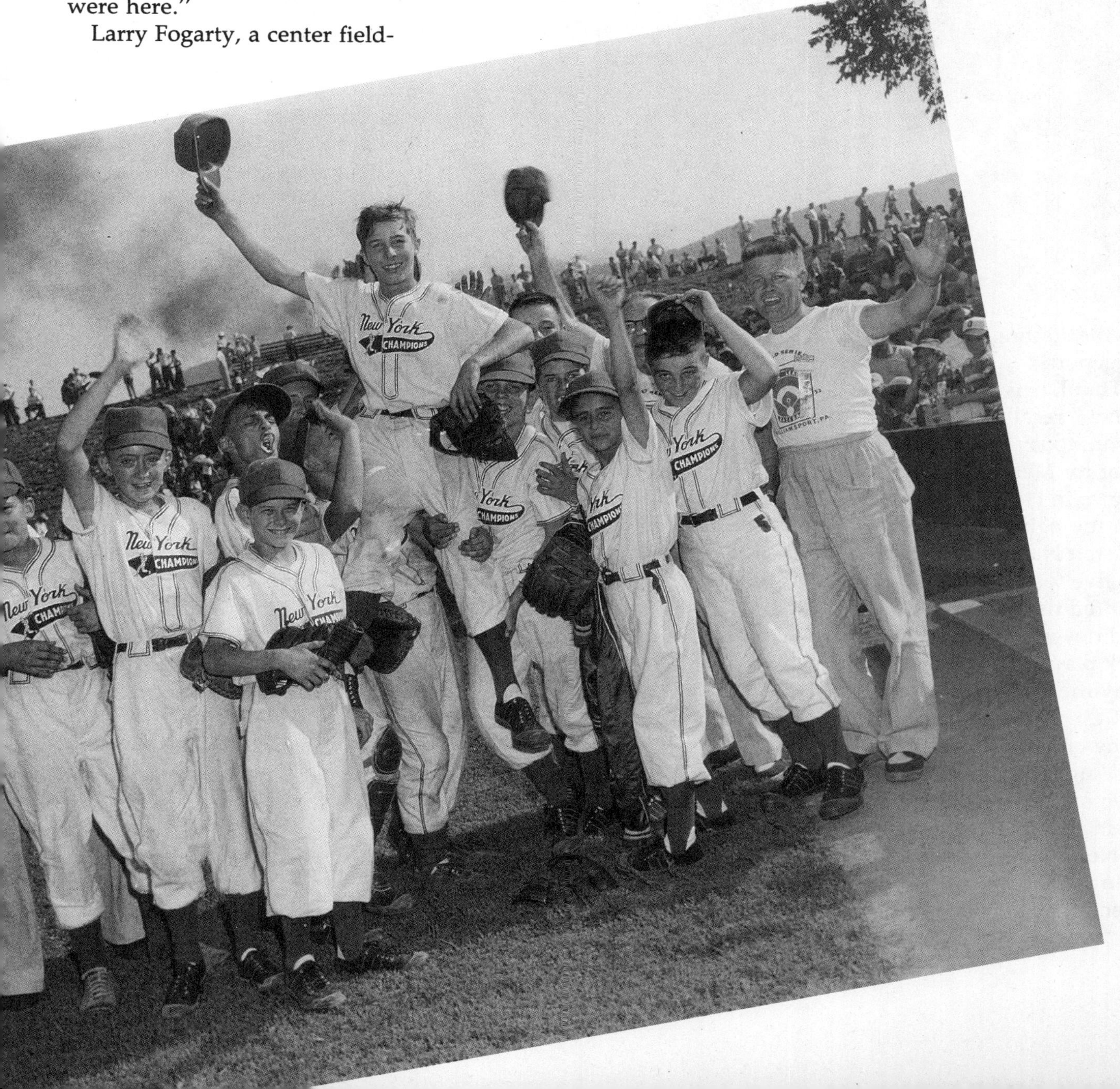

In the 1952 World Series star shortstop Richie Sacane of Monongahela (Pa.) puts his team ahead 2-0 in the first inning of the game with Hackensack (N.J.).

was the starting pitcher for Bridgeport.

"That Lewis was huge for twelve," recalled Dr. Terry Sanderson, today the medical director for Metropolitan Life Insurance in Houston but back then the right fielder for the Houston National team. "He was five feet ten inches and a hundred twenty pounds, and we'd never played against a black player before." Lewis, today the batting instructor for the St. Louis Cardinals, would be the only player on the field that August day who would move on to the major leagues, playing for the Cardinals and the New York Mets.

"In the final inning," recalled Frank Rizzo, who was umpiring at first base, "there were two outs and runners on first and third. A batter from the Texas team hit the ball to short right field. The right fielder caught it on the first bounce and threw the ball to first base. I was positioning myself for a play at second base. I called the kid safe at first base and the winning run scored." Houston wound up with a 2-1 victory in a contest that took just one hour—the shortest title game ever.

"A few days later," said Rizzo, "a photographer gave me a picture he had blown up. It showed the Texas runner's foot had not touched first base and that the ball was already in the fielder's glove."

Rizzo, one of three umpires in that game, admitted all of them were too far away from the action to make the call adequately. Little League switched to four umpires in the 1951 World Series and six became standard for the World Series in 1954. Two are selected from each of the United States regions and one from Canada and Latin America.

Dignitaries in attendance at the 1951 World Series included Notre Dame football coach Frank Leahy and baseball pitching star Schoolboy Rowe. Stamford (Ct.) edged Austin (Tex.) 3-0.

The following year Connecticut claimed its second straight Little League title as a team from Norwalk edged Monongahela (Pa.) 4-3. This was the first world series with international representation as a team from Montreal competed.

"They came to the New York State border," recalled John Lindemuth, "and the State Police picked them up there and escorted them to the Pennsylvania border. Our State Police brought them down to Williamsport. They became the toast of the town." That visit of the team from Montreal attracted much press attention and would set a pattern of hospitality and friendship in Williamsport for all foreign teams of the future.

In 1953, Joey Sims of Birmingham (Ala.) led his Southside team to a 1-0 win over Schenectady (N.Y.). Fabled baseball broadcaster Red Barber described the action for sound filming while Howard Cosell announced the play-by-play for ABC radio. James Herring was a member of the Little Rock (Ark.) team that took part in the World Series. In 1979 his son Jay would also get to the series with his Little Rock team, thus making the Herrings the only father-and-son team ever to participate in the Little League Baseball World Series.

A team from Lakeland (Fla.)

ABOVE: *The 1954 championship team from Schenectady (N.Y.) included future major leaguers John "Boog" Powell and Jim Barbieri.*

LEFT: *The team from Alabama scores in the 1953 World Series.*

came north in 1954 for the World Series competition. Three players named Powell were on the team. John "Boog" Powell was a pitcher. His brother Carl was a catcher. Another brother, Charlie, played the outfield. In the first round of play against Schenectady (N.Y.) the stocky Boog was pounded for fifteen runs in three innings.

"Jim Barbieri hit a single off me when they were already

Jim Barbieri, the smallest member of the team, played center field for the 1954 champions from Schenectady (N.Y.).

ahead four to nothing," Powell recalled. "The next batter was a kid named Bill Masucci, and he lined my first pitch over the fence and over the dike. I'll never forget watching it go."

Schenectady, aided by the play of center fielder Jim Barbieri, its smallest member, became the 1954 World Champion with a 7-5 win over Colton (Ca.).

A dozen years later "Boog" Powell and Jim Barbieri had the chance to reflect on 1954. Powell, a star for the Baltimore Orioles, and Barbieri, a member of the Los Angeles Dodgers, met in the 1966 World Series.

"I had not seen Jim since 1954," Powell remembered. "And when I saw him before that first game of the 1966 Series, we shook hands and had only a brief moment to think back on some memorable moments. I told him that we should get together someday and rehash that opening game of the World Series."

Barbieri, like Powell, also has an indelible memory of that time in 1954: "No one will ever understand the feeling unless he has the privilege of doing it himself. I'm sure the people of Schenectady still remember that day. It only seems like yesterday to me."

Ken Hubbs was another player who made it out of the 1954 Little League World Series to the major leagues. A member of the runner-up Colton team, Hubbs impressed everyone with his brilliant fielding. National League Rookie of the Year with the Chicago Cubs in 1962, Hubbs set a record for most chances accepted without error by a second baseman. A presence among his peers, a man who never forgot his Little League Baseball roots, Hubbs was killed in a plane crash after his first major league season.

In 1955, Morrisville (Pa.) battled Delaware Township (N.J.) through extra innings in the sudden-death championship game. In the bottom of the seventh inning, Richard Cominski of Morrisville came to bat with two outs. With two strikes on him, Cominski drove a fastball high and far out of the park for a home run to give his team a 4-3 win over Delaware Township—perhaps the most dramatic victory in World Series history.

Many dignitaries witnessed that taut game, including baseball immortal Cy Young, present at his fifth straight series. Young threw out the first ball and delivered this message to the Little Leaguers: "Go out and break every record in the books. Yes, break mine, too. You kids can do it. You're learning the game right and you're getting started sooner than the old-tim-

At the 1951 World Series Cy Young, the great major league pitcher who won 511 games, shares his wisdom with a Little Leaguer from San Bernardino (Ca.)

Monterrey
ICE CREAM

ers did. Though I'll never live to see it, I am certain you Little League kids of today will give us better baseball in the future than anybody ever dreamed of."

Several months later, on November 4, 1955, Cy Young, the man who won 511 games—more games than other pitcher in the history of baseball—died at the age of eighty-eight in his home in Newcomerstown, Ohio.

The first perfect game in Little League World Series history was hurled in 1956 by Fred Shapiro of Delaware Township (N.J.). But in the championship game Shapiro and his New Jersey teammates bowed to Roswell (N.M.) 3-1 before a large crowd that included Dizzy Dean, Bob Feller, and Al Schact (dubbed the "Clown Prince of Baseball" because of his antic routines).

Mexican Little League Baseball had originated in 1955. Its first league, the Aztec, was founded in Mexico City by Dr. John Niederhauser. Then the program was extended to Monterrey. In 1957, a group of twelve-year-olds from the Monterrey Industrial Little League would write one of the most inspirational and enchanting stories in all the years of the Little League World Series.

None of the youths on the Monterrey team spoke English. Most of them came from poverty-stricken homes. They played baseball in their spare time and in their bare feet. Two of the players dropped out of school because they needed to work to supplement family income. The first new clothing the members of that Monterrey team ever had was their Little League Baseball uniforms.

"At that time in the World Series competition all foreign countries had to make their way through one of the U.S. regions on their way to Williamsport," Creighton Hale explained. "The boys from Monterrey had Texas as a first stop, and the Battle of the Alamo rang out all over again. There were some strong feelings by the Texans against the kids from Mexico."

But the team from Monterrey was so good on the playing field that it won over the hearts of the Texans. And, moving north, Monterrey defeated Louisville (Ky.) to win the regional title. Wherever the Mexicans stopped, they found community support and were given food, lodging, transportation.

Much hoopla and national media attention affixed itself to the team from Monterrey all the way to Williamsport. Before Monterrey took the field in the semi-final game against Bridgeport (Ct.), it seemed everybody was rooting for them. A 2-1 triumph over Bridgeport sent Monterrey into the championship game of the World Series against La Mesa (Ca.).

The matchup was like David versus Goliath. The Californians outweighed the Mexicans by fifty pounds per player and on average were eight inches taller.

La Mesa in the 1950s was a small town in the southwest corner of California and was aptly nicknamed Little League, USA. Although its population then numbered only 30,000, everyone, including the town mascot Snoopy (a dog who retrieved more than 500 foul balls), seemed deeply involved in Little League Baseball. More than 5000 La Mesa parents helped build the town's eight

In the 1957 World Series Monterrey (Mex.) pitcher Angel Macias threw a perfect game for a 4-0 triumph against La Mesa (Ca.).

Two sluggers pose for one picture—Duke Snider and Francisco Aguiler who clinched the 1957 World Series with his hitting.

ballparks with their own hands. Local merchants competed with each other for the right to sponsor teams. The sixty-nine teams of thirteen hundred eight- to eighteen-year-olds took three hours to pass in the Little League Parade Day in La Mesa.

When fencing was needed for a new field in La Mesa, the Little Leaguers got more than they bargained for. The bricklayers' union took just one day to slap together 4200 tile blocks. Then they sent their bill: "0.00—paid in full in the fun we had." When a mountain of topsoil was needed on short notice for a new field, the La Mesans got the job done in sixteen hours. They worked through the night, using their car headlights for illumination, and the field was ready for play the next day.

When La Mesa's Little League parks were under water after thirty-two straight days of early spring rain, people feared the season would not open on time. But hundreds of fathers working long hours to pump out the water and shovel out the debris proved once again that the La Mesans always came through for Little League.

The matchup between ragtag Monterrey and tradition-rich La Mesa seemed no contest at all. Everyone agreed that if Monterrey would have any chance at all to stay with the La Mesans, it would need a big game performance from Angel Macias, its star pitcher. An ambidextrous hurler and a switch hitter, Macias proved more than equal to the challenge. He was simply dazzling as he pitched the game of his life.

Using his right arm that day for pitching and batting from the left side, Macias faced eighteen batters and struck out eleven. No ball was hit out of the infield. Macias pitched a perfect game to give Monterrey a 4-0 triumph over La Mesa, and that gritty band of boys from Monterrey became the first foreign Little League Baseball champion.

After they won the championship, the Monterrey team was taken by Bob Stirrat of Little League's Headquarters staff on a sightseeing tour of New York City. Macy's department store offered to do something special for the Mexican boys. Stirrat had turned down dozens of other similiar offers, not wanting to commercialize the Monterrey World Series triumph. However, Macy's explained that there would be no publicity, photographs, or commercialization.

The members of the Monterrey team visited the huge department store after evening hours, and each player was loaded down with new clothes and given a camera.

The boys made good use of their cameras on the next stop of their tour of the United States. Stirrat had received a phone call from President Dwight Eisenhower's press secretary, Jim Hagerty. "The President would like to see the boys before they go home," Hagerty told Stirrat. "Ike is especially taken with

the Monterrey team because his grandson is also a Little Leaguer."

So the day after their Macy's expedition, the Monterrey team went to Washington, D.C., where they took photographs of the capital's sights and of President Eisenhower. They had lunch with Vice President Richard Nixon and Senate Majority Leader Lyndon Johnson. Then it was on to Mexico City and a tumultuous heroes' welcome by more than 40,000 at the airport. For his World Series accomplishments, twelve-year-old Angel Macias was honored as Mexico's Athlete of the Year—a title generally reserved for adult sports figures.

A decade later Macias was a special guest at a Little League Congress in Houston. Creighton Hale recalled meeting him then: "I asked him 'What has been the greatest event in your life?' And he replied through an interpreter, 'The day in Washington when I met three men. One was and two were to become president of the United States.' "

In 1958, Monterrey again returned to Williamsport. Angel Macias, then thirteen, was too old to be a member of the team. But they had Hector Torres, who would be a major leaguer a decade later. Torres pitched a three-hitter against Kankakee (Ill.), enabling Monterrey to become the first team to record two consecutive World Series titles.

That 1958 championship was the last of a dozen World Series played in a Williamsport city-owned park across the street from where the teams of the Class AA Eastern League competed. Dale Long, who played for the Williamsport minor league team on his way to stardom in the majors, remembers walking across the street

LEFT: *In 1958 Monterrey (Mex.) had Hector Torres who would become a major leaguer a decade later.*

TOP RIGHT: *Winners or losers? The team from Michigan poses for a group photo at the 1959 World Series.*

BOTTOM RIGHT: *The U.S. and Canada get together at the 1959 World Series.*

to the Little League World Series games:

"Instead of the kids playing in the series wanting our autographs, we pro players wanted theirs."

The 1959 series was played in brand-new Howard J. Lamade Park. There was no grandstand then, and under a steaming August sun Art Deras, Michigan right-hander, fanned thirty of the thirty-six batters he faced in the series and shut out Auburn, (Ca.) 12-0 in the championship game. Deras also homered in the game—his thirty-third circuit clout of the 1959 season. Bobby Sunada of Auburn, the losing pitcher in the championship game, suffered his first defeat in three years of pitching in Little League Baseball.

Teams from Germany, Mexico, Canada, and Pearl Harbor (Hawaii) were part of the strong field in the 1960 series won by Levittown (Pa.) as hard-throwing Joe Mormello pitched a 5-0 no-hitter against Fort Worth (Tex.) in the finale.

In 1961 California, twice before runner-up in the title game, recorded the first in a string of three straight World Series triumphs as El Cajon defeated El Campo (Tex.). Future National Football League quarterback Brian Sipe played for the victors.

Baseball legends Ted Williams and Jackie Robinson were part of the crowd of 70,000 that came to witness the 1962 competition. Through 1962, twenty-eight states, three provinces of Canada, Puerto Rico, Mexico, France, and Germany

had sent teams to Williamsport. That year Japan made its first trip to the World Series.

"The first time the flag of the Rising Sun appeared over Lamade Stadium a lot of people were uneasy," recalled Creighton Hale. "A lot of people in Williamsport had been involved in the World War II conflict. The Japanese were also uncomfortable. They brought along their own food and medicine, and were fearful of the American doctors. However, the next time the Japanese came to Williamsport it was different. The ice had been broken and the children played together as if there had never been a World War II."

ABOVE: *In 1962 Japan made its first trip to the Little League World Series.*

RIGHT: *The 1964 champions from Staten Island (N.Y.) are honored with a tickertape parade in New York City.*

Despite the strained feelings in 1962, the kimono-garbed youngsters from Kunitachi added color and charm to the World Series festivities. But it was San Jose (Ca.) that stole the show. Behind the no-hit pitching (he came within one pitch of a perfect game) of 210-pound Ted Campbell, the Californians trimmed Kankakee (Ill.) 3-0.

Casey Stengel, one of baseball's legendary and well-traveled figures, had a connection to the Kankakee team. Back in 1910, the "old perfessor" played for a minor league team in that Illinois town. Since Kankakee finished in the red that season, Casey was "awarded" his uniform as payment for his playing efforts. It was money received by Stengel for the sale of that same uniform that Casey donated years later to start the Kankakee Little League.

A team from Izmir, Turkey, was an exotic entry in the final field in 1963. But Granada Hills (Ca.) grabbed most of the headlines, giving its state a third straight championship with a dramatic extra-inning win over Stratford (Ct.).

In 1964 Monterrey (Mexico) made it to a record third title game but lost 4-0 to Staten Island (N.Y.). Danny Yacarino, cheered on by a crowd of over 20,000 missed a perfect game by one pitch. On a 3-2 count and two outs in the final inning, he walked a batter. Even so, Danny and his friends had a lot to cheer about. Danny hurled a no-hitter and also homered. And the team from Staten Island enjoyed the thrill of a ticker-tape parade down Broadway in New York City—a fitting climax to their Little League World Series triumph.

The Monterrey (Mex.) team made it to a record third title game in 1964, but lost 4-0 to Staten Island (N.Y.).

The international nature of the World Series became even more obvious in 1965 as teams from Venezuela and Spain made first-time appearances. At the championship game many Canadian fans were on hand to cheer on Stoney Creek (Canada). They were disappointed as Windsor Locks (Ct.) prevailed over the Canadian kids with a 3-1 triumph. A 5-foot-10 181-pound first baseman, Dale Misiek (nicknamed Mount Fuji), slugged a two-run homer to supply the power of victory for the team from Connecticut.

Bill Shea, president of the Little League Foundation, threw out the ceremonial first pitch of the twentieth annual World Series. After two and one-

TOP: *A catcher gets advice from his coach at the 1965 World Series.*

BOTTOM: *The 1966 championship team from Houston (Tex.) celebrates victory.*

third innings a team from West New York (N.J.) was leading 2-0 over a powerhouse team from Houston (Tex.). Then the rains came. And the game was delayed for one hour and thirty-three minutes—the longest rain delay in series history. When play resumed, the Texans took charge and wound up with an 8-2 victory.

A sign of things to come took place at the 1967 World Series. A part of World Series competition four times before, Tokyo (Japan) defeated Chicago (Ill.) 4-1, enabling the Far East to record its first title. Superlative defensive play and a 220-foot homer by its 4-foot-9, 87-pound center fielder highlighted the victory of the team from Japan.

In 1968, Japan won its second straight championship title as Wakayama bested Richmond (Va.) 1-0. Turk Schonert, who would go on to become a quarterback for the Atlanta Falcons in the National Football League, played in that series as a member of the Garden Grove (Ca.) team. Darrell Garretson, today the National Basketball Association's supervisor of officials, was the coach of that Bolsa Little League team of Garden Grove, California. Garretson had just completed his rookie year as an NBA referee in 1968 when he volunteered his time as manager of his son Richard's team. After the series ended members of all eight teams were taken on a two-day trip to Washington. The foreign squads were given tours by their embassies and U.S. congressmen gave the American boys VIP treatment.

Baseball was introduced to Taiwan by the Japanese in the years 1895-1945, when it was a colony. In the years after World War II, the sport went into a decline there. Little League Baseball was introduced into Taiwan in the early 1960s. In 1968, a highly regarded team of boys from Japan was trounced by a group of aborigine boys from a mountain village in Taiwan. The Taiwanese boys had learned how to play baseball using sticks and stones in place of bats and balls. They learned well.

In 1969, in its first year of international Little League competition, Taiwan gave the Far East its third straight title when the Golden Dragons of Taipei Little League defeated Santa Clara (Ca.) 5-0 in the 1969

In the 1967 World Series, Tokyo (Japan) defeated Chicago (Ill.) enabling the Far East to record its first title.

championship game. Carney Lansford, now with the Oakland As, played for Santa Clara. Because of the time-zone differences it was nightfall when news of the victory reached Taiwan. Thousands had remained up throughout the night to listen to the play-by-play broadcast direct form Williamsport. All over Taiwan the sound of exploding firecrackers mixed with the sight of thousands of unfurling red-and-gold banners. It was a victory celebration that would be repeated many times in the years ahead.

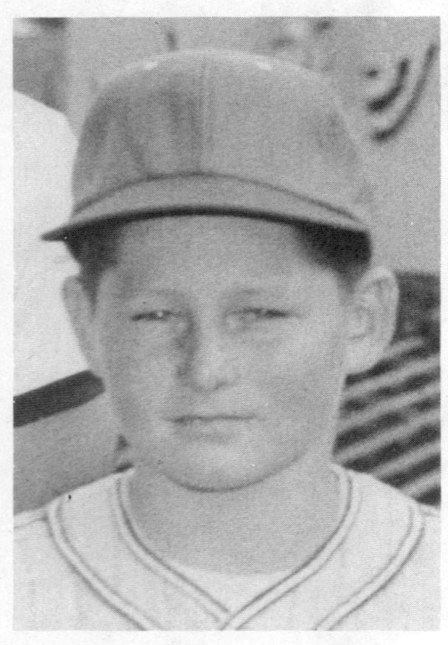

Carney Lansford, now with the Oakland As, played with Santa Clara in the 1969 World Series, but his team lost to Taiwan.

The championship game in 1970 between a team from Wayne (N.J.) and a team from Campbell (Ca.) guaranteed that for the first time since 1966 a United States team would win the Little League World Series. Wayne recorded a 2-0 triumph to take that title.

In 1971, a team from Gary (Ind.)—the first all-black team in World Series competition—was matched in the championship game against Tainan (Taiwan). Hundreds of Gary residents made their way to Williamsport to cheer on their team.

"The hit of the series," in the words of the late Ray Keyes, sports editor of the *Williamsport Sun-Gazette*, "was Kenny (Squeaky) Hayes. At 4-foot-5.5 inches and 62 pounds, he was the smallest player there.

"Bouncing around the third base coaching box like a major leaguer," Keyes recalled, "Squeaky would put his hands on his hips to start an inning. Next he'd give the sign. He'd look pretty dejected if a batter didn't follow his signal. He'd use both hands to illustrate how a batter should swing."

One batter who didn't need much instruction on how to swing was Gary's Lloyd McClendon. In five official at-bats in the series, he homered each time on the first pitch.

McClendon, who would go on to play for the Cincinnati Reds and Chicago Cubs, was the pitcher in the championship game against Taiwan. In his

first at-bat he blasted a towering 220-foot, three-run home run, giving Gary the early lead in the game.

"Believe me," McClendon said, "I was scared when we played the Taiwanese. Especially after I hit the home run. But all they did after that was not let me hit. They walked me three times intentionally. I didn't like it when they walked me and neither did the crowd there"—McClendon still recalls the feeling. "I wanted a chance to hit."

Through the first nine innings McClendon allowed just three hits and three runs, and the game moved into the ninth tied 3-3. Yielding two walks and a single, an exhausted McClendon removed himself

from the game. Taiwan sent fourteen batters to the plate in the ninth inning, scored nine runs, and romped to a 12-3 triumph in the longest championship game in World Series history, two hours and fifty-one minutes.

The two hundredth game in World Series history was played in 1972 in its twenty-sixth year; it pitted a team from San Juan (Puerto Rico) against a club from Windsor (Ontario). However, both teams were on the sidelines for the championship game. Taipei Little League was again in the winner's circle after shutting out Hammond (Ind.) 6-0 to win the title game.

In 1972 and 1973 Taiwan steamrolled the competition once again. A 12-0 romp over Cactus Little League of Tucson (Ariz.) gave Tainan City the 1973 title. That Taiwan team was used to scoring runs in batches, having set a World Series record in 1973 by recording twenty-seven runs in a game against Tampa, Florida.

Another team representing the Far East, Kao Ksiung, making its first World Series appearance, racked up twelve runs and easily defeated Red Bluff (Ca.) in 1974. It was the third time in four years that a Taiwanese team scored a dozen runs in a World Series championship game. Gale Gilbert, who would become a quarterback for the NFL's Seattle Seahawks, was a member of that Red Bluff team.

ABOVE LEFT: *In the first top finish by a U.S. team since 1966, the Wayne (N.J.) team won the 1970 World Series.*

ABOVE RIGHT: *In 1971, a team from Gary (Ind.)—the first all-black team in World Series competition—faced tough opposition from Taiwan.*

The 1975 title game was a tug of war between Belmont Little League of Tampa (Fla.) and a team from Lakewood (N.J.) that had come from behind in game after game to get to the championship contest. The New Jersey team trailed 2-0 after the first inning as Tampa scored on a two-run homer. It was to be the Florida team's only hit of the game. Lakewood's pitcher Bobby DelConte, in his only start of tournament play, reached back to keep Tampa at bay. With two outs in the bottom of the sixth inning, the Floridians had the tying run on first base. DelConte had a 1-2 count on the batter. And then, in what DelConte later described as the pitch of his life ("I knew it was my last inning in Little League"), he fired the ball to the plate. Strikeout!

"That seventy-five team I can describe in one word, and that's awesome," said Steve Belitrand, who co-managed it along with Richard Work. "It's something you always want to remember," he continued. Sixty-eight hundred teams started. We were there at the end. Seven weeks. Fifteen victories. Six championships."

In 1976 the thirtieth Little League Baseball World Series saw the Chofu team of Tokyo defeat Campbell (Ca.) 10-3 to

In the 1975 World Series the Lakewood (N.J.) team came from behind, as they had done game after game, to defeat the Belmont Heights Little League of Tampa (Fla.).

give Japan its third championship. The players on that victorious Chofu team bent down on the base paths and scooped up earth into pots and baseball caps to collect some Williamsport soil to take home as a memento of their World Series triumph. Baseball immortals Ernie Banks, Bob Gibson, and Joe DiMaggio were on the sidelines. The Yankee Clipper told everyone, "I have a warm spot in my heart for Little League." And then he listened patiently as an eleven-year-old asked him to autograph a baseball.

DiMaggio put his arm around the youngster's shoulder. "How would you like me to sign—Yankee Clipper?"

"No, please " the boy looked up at DiMaggio. "Just sign it 'To Mike, from Mr. Coffee.' "

The years 1977 to 1981 saw World Series play again dominated by teams from Taiwan. Li-Teh defeated El Cajon (in 1977). The following year Pingtung City romped 11-1 over San Ramon Valley of Danville (Ca.). So enamored was Pingtung with the treatment its team received that it proclaimed itself a sister city of Williamsport. A delegation of Williamsporters including the mayor was invited to Pingtung City as official guests in a show of international accord. Daniel P. Kirby, then mayor of Williamsport, established so much rapport with the Taiwanese that they named a Little League Baseball field in Tapei in his honor.

Taiwan's love affair with Little League Baseball is a serious matter. Their program is operated by top executives. In the early years of their Little League involvement a top-ranking Taiwanese political figure brought their team over to Williamsport. In the years since, outstanding businessmen have accompanied the team. The present host is P. P. Tang, president of the Broadcast Companyof China.

Each team, on returning from the World Series in Williamsport, had been met by General Chiang Kai-shek. "It was his way of showing his interest in the sport," noted Creighton Hale. "When Chiang's son succeeded him," Hale continued, "the same ritual was followed."

On one of Hale's visits to Taiwan he was asked to lay a wreath at the foot of a statue of Chiang Kai-shek. "Everything

In 1976 the Chofu team of Tokyo defeated Campbell (Ca.) 10-3 to give Japan its third championship.

was in Chinese during the ceremony," remembered Hale, "so I didn't really have an awareness of what was going on. But at the end of the ceremony, they announced in English that the gentleman who laid the wreath was the president of Little League Baseball. There was a lot of applause. Most of the people there did not understand English, but they understood the words Little League Baseball—that phrase is an international language."

The thirty-third Little League World Series, in 1979, saw a Campbell (Ca.) team in the finals for the third time in the 1970s. In 1970 they were nicknamed the Cardiac Kids. By 1976 they were referred to as the Campbell Kids. The 1979 entry was called the Campbell Clones because the players on that team were all light-haired, about five feet tall, and weighed about a hundred pounds.

Campbell's competition was a talented team from Pu-tzu Town (Taiwan). "The Taiwanese kids," recalled Subby Agliolo of Campbell, "towered over

Before: A Central division runner leaps at home plate in the preliminary rounds of the 1978 World Series.

us. I thought they were just awesome and that we were ten runs down before the game started.''

Through seven innings of intense baseball the teams battled each other out for out, run for run. Going into the eighth, the score was tied 1-1. ''I still get goosepimples thinking about it,'' Agliolo said.

''For sheer enjoyment,'' legendary baseball broadcaster Red Barber remembered, ''I can't recall anything to top that game. Those kids—you could feel it from the broadcasting booth—enjoyed playing the game. It was a joy to watch the way they played. They would throw to the right base and make the right play at the right time.''

In the bottom of the eighth inning, a run-scoring single with two outs by Hou Chia-mou gave Pu-tzu Town Little League a 2-1 triumph and the world championship. Pitcher Dai Han-chao was magnificent. He pitched a no-hitter and struck out seventeen.

In 1980, Belmont Heights, a team from a virtually all-black neighborhood in Tampa (Fla.)

After: The same player (see previous page) lands on home plate. Is he safe or out? It's your call.

12

made it on the championship game. They faced the highly disciplined Hualian (Taiwan) Little Leaguers, who had slugged seven home runs in a game to set a Little League World Series record. The Taiwan team defeated Belmont Heights by one run in the final game of the World Series.

The following year the team from Tampa went undefeated in twenty-eight regular season games and survived the playoff competition. Once again Belmont Heights faced a team from Taiwan with the world championship on the line. In a toughly contested game, Tai-chung (Tawain) prevailed.

"We may not be champions of the world," "Dad" Wilson, coach of the Tampa team, said, "but we know we've got the right stuff and you can't take that away."

A few days later there was a parade and motorcade as ten U.S. Army jeeps carried the players and coaches of Belmont Heights Little League through the streets of Tampa.

"I watched the people waving to us as we rode around the street," recalled Derek Bell, who pitched in that championship game, "black people, white people, everybody cheering. It didn't really hit me that we were the national Little League Baseball champions and that we would never play together as a team until I looked into the eyes of a little boy standing on the sidewalk. He was waving and his eyes were filled with tears. Something went through me. I don't know why, but that sight made that moment real for me."

Going into the 1982 World Series, no U.S. team had won the championship since 1975, a year no foreign teams competed. Taiwan had a stranglehold on the title. Their teams had not lost a game in World Series competition since 1970. Their 1982 entry, Pu-tzu Town, was highly favored to give Taiwan its sixth straight title.

It didn't work out that way. Behind Cody Webster, a husky pitcher who featured a seventy-five-mile-per-hour fast ball and a "drop-curve," Kirkland (Wash.) National Little League defeated the team from Taiwan in one of the most exciting World Series in history. How-

In the 1981 World Series, Belmont Heights of Tampa (Fla.) came to Williamsport undefeated (28-0) to lose to Taiwan in the final.

ever, when the game began, it did not look like it would turn out the way it did. Webster gave up a walk and went to a full count on virtually every batter he faced in the first inning, although he did manage to strike out the side.

The pressure on the two teams kept building. Frank Rizzo, umpiring behind the plate as he has been for every championship game since 1960, recalled the time: "The United States hadn't won in quite a while. There were chants: 'U.S.A., U.S.A' The fans were on their feet most of their time. Taiwan always had the potential to score a lot of runs in a hurry, so the crowd got louder and louder with each out in the sixth and final inning. The game ended with a called third strike. Boy, I still can remember that moment."

"I really wanted to win bad," Cody Webster recalled. "And I knew we could do it. I began to concentrate on the catcher's glove instead of everything else that was happening, and from then on I was all right."

He was more than all right. Cody Webster, the kid with floppy blond hair and an All-American name, was superb. He allowed just two singles, struck out a dozen batters, and slugged a towering 285-foot home run over the center-field fence—the longest in series history—to cap Kirkland's 6-0 triumph. That ball was caught by a Williamsport youth named Dave Bennett. After the game, Bennett caught up with Cody and gave the ball to him. "I figured Cody would want to have it," he said.

The Pu-tzu town team showed excellent sportsmanship. Its players wouldn't leave the field until they had the chance to rush over and congratulate the Kirkland players. As they shook the hands of the new champions, Taiwanese coach Chung Sing-fa said, "We will come back. Kirkland is a really good team. That is why they won. We didn't come up to our level, which has never happened before."

"The Pu-tzu team took the defeat like proud young men," Rizzo recalled. "That's one reason why I have stayed in this program so long, because of moments like that."

More than 40,000 people showed up at a victory celebration in Seattle for the 1982 Little League World Champs, a team that went through sixteen games of tournament competition and the series and won them all. Much of the attention was given to the boy whose name seemed to have come straight out of a Zane Grey western—Cody Webster, modest and mature in his moment in the spotlight.

"We have a lot of good players," Cody told the cheering

crowds. "It was the whole team that won this. All fourteen of us are important."

Pierre Turgeon, who would become the first player selected in the 1982 National Hockey League draft, played in that 1982 World Series as a member of the Rouyn team that came from a small lumbering and mining town in northwestern Quebec.

In 1983, Europe according to Little League Baseball's playoff structure, was represented by Saudi Arabia—the first time a team from that nation had participated in the series. The squad was made up primarily of American youngsters whose parents worked in the oil and aircraft industries in Saudi Arabia. A team from Osaka (Japan) also made its first appearance marking the first time since 1976 that the Far East representative was not from Taiwan.

East Marietta (Ga.) faced Barahona (Dominican Republic) in the championship game—it was also the first time for those teams in the World Series. "There was a feeling among us," recalled Ken Carlson, a member of East Marietta, "that something was being shared. It kept on building. Before, a lot of the families didn't know each other, but as the team got closer and closer to Williamsport, the closer we all got."

On August 27, a 4-foot-11, 86-pound center fielder began the rally that enabled his team from East Marietta to score a 3-1 victory over the Liquito Hernandez Little League of Barahona and win the thirty-seventh World Series. It was only the second time the United States had won consecutive titles in the World Series since 1965 and 1966.

For Dickie Thomas, a coach on that team from Georgia, that moment "was a once-in-a-lifetime thing for me. I feel like the luckiest man in the world to be part of it." And white-bearded Richard Hilton, manager of that 1983 championship team, who was going to retire from coaching at age fifty, going to get a younger man to do it," admitted after the Georgia triumph, "I can't now. I just can't."

Another team from the South made it to the championship game in 1984, but Altamonte Springs (Fla.) lost 6-2 to Seoul (Korea) Little League. It was the first time a Korean team had won the Series.

In 1984 Brussels (Belgium) competed in the World Series for the first time. To get to Williamsport, Brussels had to defeat teams from the Hague (The Netherlands), Torrejon (Spain), Geilenkirchen (West Germany), London (England), Alkhobar (Saudi Arabia), and Naples (Italy). It also broke new ground by including a girl on its team roster. Victoria Roche, a reserve outfielder on that 1984

The runner dives for home in the 1984 World Series, which was the first to see a roster, for the European championship team, include a girl player.

European championship team, received a lot of attention and posed a small problem. There were no facilities for girls in the cabin complex that houses World Series teams. So Victoria wound up staying in a nearby hotel with the wife and daughter of the Belgian team's manager.

In 1985, in the first day of the five-day sudden-death showdown at Lamade Stadium, Maracaibo (Venezuela) knew it was in a survival contest against powerful Seoul, the defending champion. Seoul's route to the championship game came via victories over two Korean teams and squads from Guam, Indonesia, Japan, Taiwan, the Philippines, and Hong Kong. A picture-perfect swing by Seoul's Kyung-hwan Cho sent a fast ball thrown by Venezuela's Oswaldo Villalobos 204 feet over the outfield fence for a home run.

Tears streamed down the face of the Venezuelan, but he still had the composure and the sportsmanship to trot over to the Korean, running out his home run. The dejected youth

Pictured here is the camera that transmits live color action from the mask of the home-plate umpire. Frank Rizzo, in 1985, was the first to wear it.

from Venezuela shook the Korean's hand.

"To me, that's what Little League is all about," said Mickey Cioffi, one of the "uncles" who host visiting teams. "Kids learn to get along with each other, to accept victory and also defeat. And if you're wondering about Villalobos' feelings, well, about a half-hour later he was smiling and laughing again. Kids have a way of bouncing back."

That 1985 World Series marked the first time a championship game did not include a United States team. Mexicali (Mexico), which had competed in the U.S.A. Western Region for fifteen years, played in the final game as a kind of surrogate United States team. Seoul won again, however, defeating Mexicali 7-1 in a game that saw ABC-TV and Little League Baseball combine efforts to make history.

On August 24, 1985, American baseball fans, for the first time ever, saw live color pictures transmitted from a camera on the mask of home-plate umpire Frank Rizzo. The microminiature color camera, about the size of a golfball and weighing four ounces, "didn't affect my ability to call the pitches at all," Rizzo said.

The umpire was also equipped with an ultraminiature video transmitter, weighing about five pounds, mounted on a specially designed belt. The transmitter sent the pictures from the camera to a receiving site behind home plate.

According to Dennis Lewin, coordinating producer of ABC's "Wide World of Sports" and producer of ABC's Little League World Series coverage, development of the unusual camera "enables the viewer at home to be part of the live action from the umpire's point of view."

In 1986 Ray Keyes, who covered forty-two consecutive World Series since the beginning and Putsee Vannucci, on the scene as Little League photographer from the start, tossed out the ceremonial first pitches. The town of Brunswick, Maine, sent over a thousand supporters to cheer on its team. Others in the final eight included: Tucson (Ariz.), Sarasota (Fla.) Norridge (Ill.), Tainan Park (Taiwan), Valleyfield (Quebec), Madrid (Spain), and Maracaibo (Venezuela). When it was all over, another powerhouse from the Far East scored a one-sided victory in the championship game. Tainan Park shut out Tucson 12-0.

A crowd of 35,000 attended the fortieth-anniversary World Series in 1987. That series also hosted a reunion for members of the original Maynard championship team of 1947. Manager Charlie Scuder and Coach Harry Berry were reunited with their players, many of whom they had not seen in forty years.

The Reverend Edward Younken, a Presbyterian minister in East Rutherford, New Jersey, delivered the invocation during the ceremonies. Younken pitched the first no-hitter in Little League history in Wil-

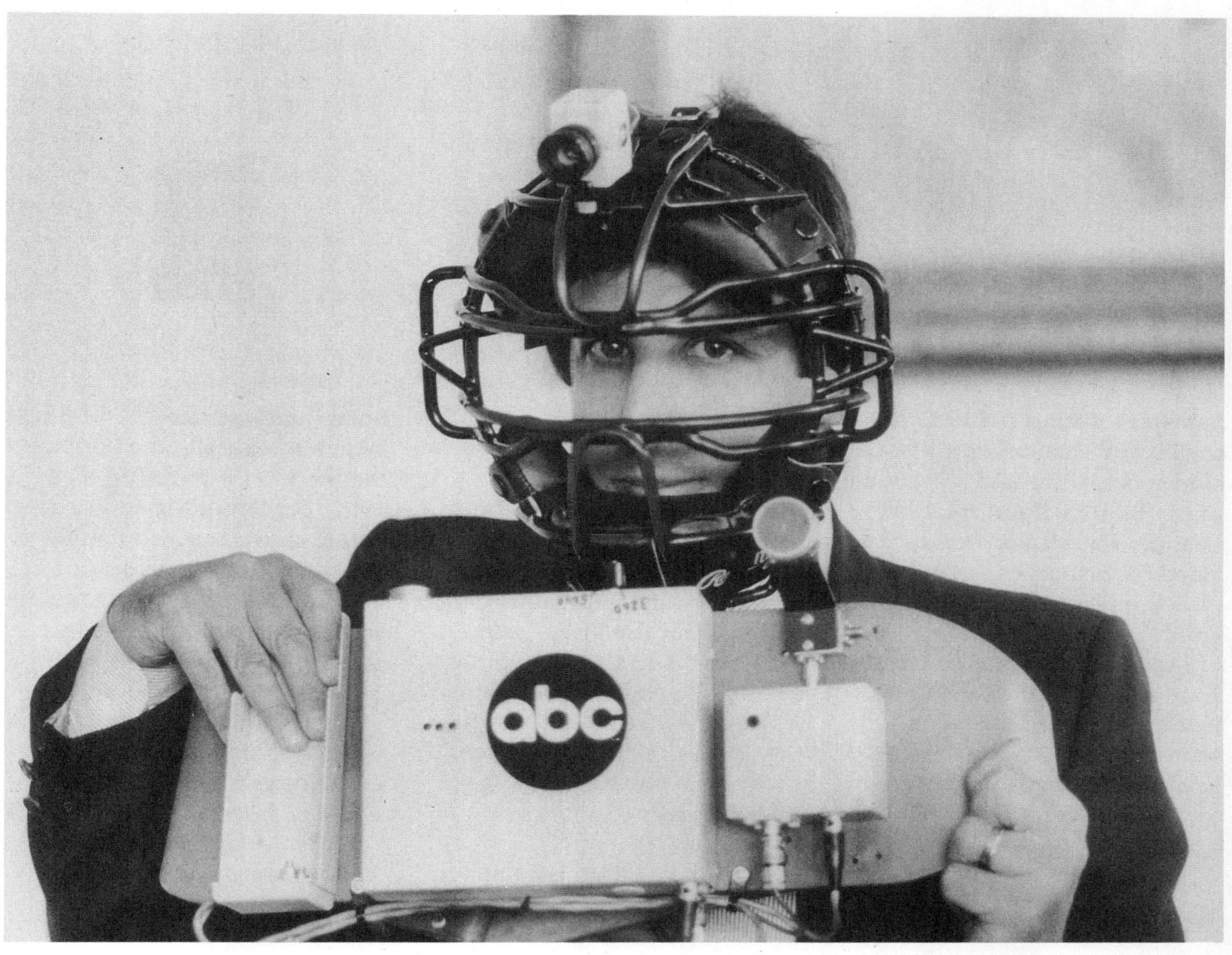
abc

liamsport during the 1942 season. Brent Musburger, television sportscaster and a graduate of the Billings (Mont.) Little League, was also on hand. "I decided," Musburger said, "to visit the place I dreamed of as a child."

Hua Lian (Taiwan) trounced Irvine (Ca.) 21-1 in the most lopsided championship-game score ever. It was the Far East's seventeenth win in twenty-one years and Taiwan's twelfth championship in fourteen World Series appearances.

Pan Yu-long powered Taiwan's scoring with a pair of home runs, one a grand slam. Aron Garcia yielded all twenty-one runs for the losers before his father, Bob Garcia, who was also the manager of the Irvine team, finally removed him from the game.

"Things sure have changed here," said Jack Losch, who had been a member of the original Maynard championship team in 1947. For Frank Rizzo, things had changed but also remained the same. Rizzo was behind the plate for the 1987 championship game—still on the scene as an umpire as he had been in 1947.

For Rizzo, as for the other volunteer umpires involved in Little League Baseball tournaments, there is no reimbursement for expenses, no payment of any kind. "It's considered an honor to be chosen to work," noted Rizzo.

In 1970, Shunzi Nagasaka of Tokyo became the first Far Eastern umpire to work the World Series games. In the intervening years, umpires have traveled from Canada, Puerto Rico, Guam, and virtually all of the fifty United States to fulfill their dream of working in the Series. the final twelve selected for the Little League World Series in Williamsport generally average about twenty years experience per umpire.

Sometimes even a celebrity could be found in the unexpected role of umpire. Alvy Moore, famous for his portrayal of Hank Kimble, county farm agent in the popular Television series *Green Acres,* officiated at second base in a series game in the early 1970s. Moore got his start as an umpire in Toluca Lake Little League in his home town of North Hollywood, California, in the late 1950s.

"When I first started," Moore recalled, "nobody wanted to be an umpire. So I signed on. When I worked a real game for the first time there was a rhubarb between another ump and a manager. I didn't know any better then, so I just walked over and said 'It looked to me like the kid was out.' The manager wasn't too pleased. He turned to me and said 'Who asked you?'

"That experience," Moore said, "made me realize how important knowing all the ins and outs of umpiring are." That realization was the spur that sent Moore to umpire school in Williamsport. The likable Moore became so proficient at officiating that he became umpire-in-chief of Toluca Lake Little League. So when he was given the chance to umpire in the world Series at Williamsport it was not a case of his being given the job because of his celebrity status. Moore had qualified for the role.

"In that 1976 game between California and Japan," Moore reminisced. "I made a call that I'll never forget. I was working second base. The kid from California hit a slow roller to the shortstop, who didn't really throw to second—he sort of tossed it. There was no sound from the second baseman's glove. But I happened to be in the right position. The ball got there before the runner. Out!

"At that point the California manager came out onto the field to confer with me and Frank Rizzo, the home-plate umpire. I explained that I was in the perfect spot at the right time to make the play. That was that. I've always dreaded making a bad call against a Little Leaguer. Imagine how I would have felt if I'd done it during a World Series. As it was, I hated to call that 'out' against my home state of California."

The forty-second Little League World Series championship game on August 27, 1988, before a crowd of 33,000 and an ABC-TV audience estimated at 20 million saw the Far East claim its fifth straight title. Chen-lung Yu's one-hitter and Wei-chih Chen's four-for-four day including a three-run homer boosted Tai Chung (Taiwan) to a 10-0 triumph over Pearl City (Hawaii).

000
000
ANDOVER

In pregame activities Dr. Creighton Hale named the working press area in Lamdae Stadium the Ray Keyes Press Section in honor of the sports editor of the *Williamsport Sun-Gazette*, the only sports writer to have covered all of the series since the first one.

Orel Hershiser and Tom Seaver both tossed out commemorative first pitches to Bill Shea, president of the Little League Foundation. Hershiser was in attendance as his parents were honored as Little League Parents of the Year.

Seaver, who played in his first Little League game in 1953 in Fresno, California, was announced as the first member of the Peter J. McGovern Museum's Hall of Fame for Distinguished Little League Graduates.

"Today," Dr. Hale said in his presentation to Seaver, "Little League Baseball would like to thank Tom for so many memorable baseball moments, but an even deeper thanks for providing millions of aspiring Little Leaguers with a consistent, positive role model."

In 1988, Tom Seaver (facing right), with Dr. Creighton Hale (facing left), became the first inductee to the Peter J. McGovern Museum's Hall of Fame.

LITTLE LEAGUE WORLD SERIES CHAMPIONSHIP GAMES AND SCORES

Year	Team	Score
1947	Maynard, Williamsport, Pennsylvania	16
	Lock Haven, Pennsylvania	7
1948	Lock Haven, Pennsylvania	6
	St. Petersburg, Florida	5
1949	Hammonton, New Jersey	5
	Pensacola, Florida	0
1950	Houston, Texas	2
	Bridgeport, Connecticut	1
1951	Stamford, Connecticut	3
	Austin, Texas	0
1952	Norwalk, Connecticut	4
	Monongahela, Pennsylvania	3
1953	Birmingham, Alabama	1
	Schenectady, New York	0

All eyes focus on the play at home plate at the 1953 Little League World Series.

1954	Schenectady, New York	7
	Colton, California	5
1955	Morrisville, Pennsylvania	4
	Delaware Township, New Jersey	3
1956	Roswell, New Mexico	3
	Delaware Township, New Jersey	1
1957	Monterrey, Mexico	4
	La Mesa, California	0
1958	Monterrey, Mexico	10
	Kankakee, Illinois	1
1959	Hamtramck, Michigan	12
	Auburn, California	0
1960	Levittown, Pennsylvania	5
	Fort Worth, Texas	0
1961	El Cajon, California	4
	El Campo, Texas	2
1962	San Jose, California	3
	Kankakee, Illinois	0
1963	Granada Hills, California	2
	Stratford, Connecticut	1

ABOVE: *A Pacific division player heads to take his turn at bat in the 1958 World Series. Note that wooden bats were still in use then.*

RIGHT: *The 1960 champions from Levittown, Pennsylvania hoist up one of their star players.*

ABOVE: *New York City salutes the 1964 Little League champions from Staten Island with a tickertape parade.*

RIGHT: *Baseball great Casey Stengel poses with Little Leaguers at the 1964 World Series.*

1964	Mid Island, Staten Island, New York	4
	Obispado, Monterrey, Mexico	0
1965	Windsor Locks, Connecticut	3
	Stoney Creek, Ontario	1
1966	Westbury American, Houston, Texas	3
	American, West New York, New Jersey	2
1967	West Tokyo, Japan	4
	North Roseland, Chicago, Illinois	1
1968	Wakayama, Japan	1
	Richmond, Virginia	0
1969	Taipei, Taiwan	5
	Santa Clara, California	0
1970	American, Wayne, New Jersey	2
	Campbell, California	0
1971	Tainan, Taiwan	12
	Anderson, Gary, Indiana	3
1972	Taipei, Taiwan	6
	Hammond, Indiana	0
1973	Tainan City, Taiwan	12
	Cactus, Tucson, Arizona	0
1974	Kao Ksiung, Taiwan	12
	Red Bluff, California	1

These smiling faces belong to two players on the 1967 championship team from West Tokyo, Japan.

Ted Williams offers his best wishes to a player at the 1968 World Series.

1975	Lakewood, New Jersey	4
	Belmont Heights, Tampa, Florida	3
1976	Chofu, Tokyo, Japan	10
	Campell, California	3
1977	Li-teh, Taiwan	7
	El Cajon, California	2
1978	Pin-kuang, Pin-tung, Taiwan	11
	San Ramon Valley, Danville, California	1
1979	Pu-tzu Town, Taiwan	2
	Campbell, California	1
1980	Long Kuong, Hua Lian, Taiwan	4
	Belmont Heights, Tampa, Florida	3
1981	Tai-chung, Taiwan	4
	Belmont Heights, Tampa, Florida	2
1982	Kirkland National, Kirkland, Washington	6
	Pu-tzu town, Taiwan	0
1983	East Marietta National, Marietta, Georgia	3
	Liquito Hernandez, Barahona, Dominican Republic	1
1984	Seoul National, Seoul, Korea	6
	Altamonte Springs, Florida	2
1985	Seoul National, Seoul, Korea	7
	Mexicali, Mexico	1
1986	Tainan Park, Taiwan	12
	International, Tucson, Arizona	0
1987	Hua Lin, Taiwan	21
	Irvine, California	1
1988	Tai Chung, Chinese Taipei,	10
	Pearl City, Hawaii	1

Pre-game ceremonies at the 1986 World Series Championship.

A vital part of the support structure that makes Little League Baseball possible, the volunteer umpires for the 1960 World Series join the salute to the flag.

LEFT: A determined-looking third baseman from Tampa, Florida, is ready for anything that may come his way at the 1981 World Series.

BOTTOM: Canadian Little Leaguers patiently join in the pre-game ceremonies at the Little League World Series.

RIGHT: A Latin American pitcher in the 1987 Little League World Series stares down the opposition.

14

SOUTH
LITTLE LEAGUE BASEBALL
LITTLE LEAGUE
1966
WORLD CHAMPIONS

LITTLE LEAGUE
West
WORLD SERIES
WEST

LEFT TOP: The 1966 Little League World Series champions, the Westbury Little League from Houston, Texas, display the badges of victory.

LEFT BOTTOM: Little Leaguers from California express confidence that they are "number one."

RIGHT: Batter up! A Stamford, Connecticut, Little Leaguer takes his turn in the batter's box.

BOTTOM: A Little Leaguer from Barrington, Illinois, heads for home in the 1981 World Series game against the Belmont Heights Little League from Tampa, Florida.

LEFT: The Little League World Series promotes international good will as children transcend language barriers to become friends and play baseball.

BOTTOM: The Belmont Heights Little Leaguers, from Tampa, Florida, celebrate the game-winning homerun in the 1981 Little League World Series.

RIGHT TOP: A Latin American batter faces a European pitcher in the 1986 Little League World Series.

RIGHT BOTTOM: Little Leaguers from Pearl City, Hawaii, await the start of the 1988 Little League World Series championship game.

AMERICA

LITTLE LEAGUE
WORLD SERIES

Little League
WORLD SERIES
WILLIAMSPORT
USA
PENNA.

PRECEEDING PAGES: The Little League World Series hot air balloon takes off prior to the beginning of the championship game.

TOP: Following a Far East tradition, teammates toss the winning pitcher in the air at the 1981 Little League World Series.

LEFT: Nothing can faze this participant in the Little League Softball World Series at Kalamazoo, Michigan.

RIGHT: Little Leaguers display the exuberance that typifies the team introductions at the Little League World Series.

17

TOP: Youngsters from Latin America listen intently to their manager's instructions.

LEFT: A Little Leaguer takes a swing at the ball during World Series play.

TOP RIGHT: The Darlington Little League from Pawtucket, Rhode Island, congratulates its homerun hitter at the 1980 Little League World Series.

BOTTOM RIGHT: Fans from Spring, Texas, show their spirit at the 1988 Little League World Series.

TEXAS

ABOVE: Little Leaguers huddle with their coach, showing the team unity that is the key to Little League's success.

TOP RIGHT AND LEFT: Pin trading is gaining in popularity with each succeeding World Series.

BOTTOM RIGHT: Young players from the Far East collect infield dirt at Howard J. Lamade Stadium where the Little League World Series is played each year. They take the dirt home as a treasured souvenir.

ABOVE: A Far East player slides into homeplate.

RIGHT: Dugout, the Little League Baseball mascot, and the Philly Phanatic, the mascot of the Philadelphia Phillies, share a moment together at the Little League World Series.

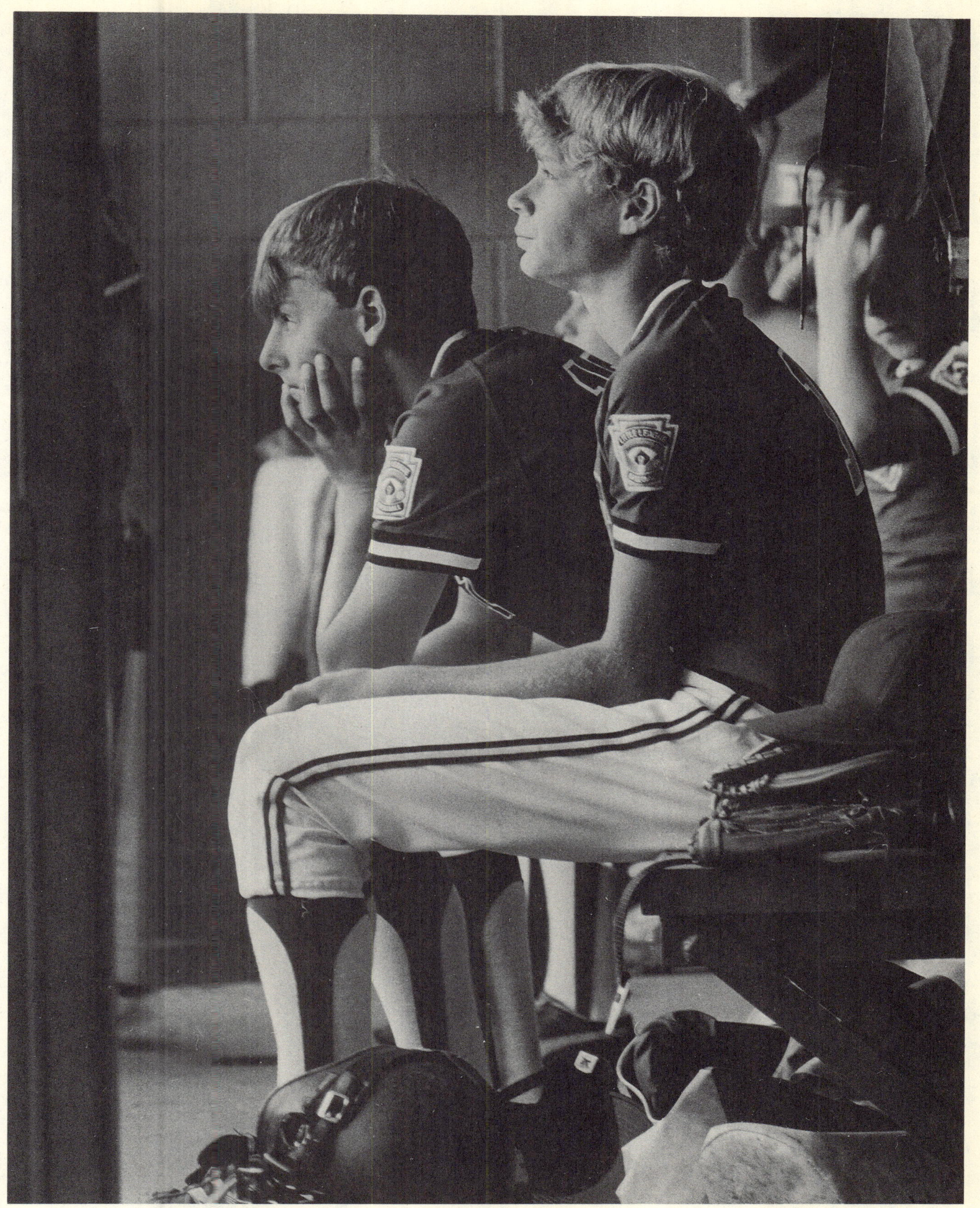

Determination and concentration at the 1968 World Series.

Sideline Champions

From that very first day in the summer of 1939 when Carl Stotz pledged to his nephews that he would work out a plan for a league, Little League Baseball has relied on the efforts and contributions of volunteers. It began as a community project involving only a handful of adult supporters. It has grown into an international program involving virtually millions of people. But it still remains a grass-roots operation run by a cadre of 750,000 dedicated volunteers.

"The amazing thing about the entire Little League program is that it depends so much on volunteers," said William Shea, himself an unpaid volunteer who has functioned as a trustee since 1960 and president of the Little League Foundation since 1976, when he succeeded James A. Farley, former postmaster general of the United States. "For the numbers involved, Little League has a very small professional and administrative staff and runs on a surprisingly modest budget. This is because the backbone of the program is its army of volunteers: the coaches, the managers, the umpires, the district administrators. They deserve all the credit in the world."

Credit has been officially

Little League means as much to its thousands of volunteers as to its players.

A coach offers valuable advice to a player from California.

given to a microcosm of the multitudes who have served Little League Baseball so well through its first fifty years. "Since 1958, we have presented a distinguished service award to an outstanding volunteer at each of our congresses," said Stephen Keener, public relations director. "In 1984, after the retirement of Peter J. McGovern, it was decided the award was an appropriate living memorial for the man under whose tenure as president and chairman of the board Little League grew tenfold. So it is now known as the Peter J. McGovern Distinguished Service Award."

Recipients of the award are:

Recipient	*Year of Award*
Arnold White	1958
Perry Winstead	1960
Harris Plaisted	1961
Nick Aromandi	1963
Joe Eckert	1965
Art Mikelsen	1967
Bill Robertson	1969
Faith Columbo	1971
Pat Knight	1973
Ellen Porterfield	1975
Lucky Porterfield	1975
Y. Hada	1978
H. Taylor Bell	1981
James B. Whittington	1984
Milton F. Ziehn	1987

Dr. Luke LaPorta has sat on the board of directors of Little League since 1972 and has been chairman of the board since 1983—both are volunteer positions. Back in 1950 LaPorta, a high school athletic director, started the first Little League in central New York State—the Liverpool Little League. Then, like a modern-day Johnny Appleseed, with other volunteers he set up about sixty leagues in that region: "It was like spreading seeds to the wind."

"I was in China a couple of years ago as a guest of its Sports Federation," LaPorta continued, "and I realized that when

Many adults who get involved in Little League as parents stay on after their children are grown.

they think of coaching over there, they think of someone who is a professional, someone who is trained and paid to coach. It was very difficult for me to explain to them that none of our Little League coaches are paid. They could not understand the concept of a volunteer. Yet there would be no Little League without volunteers. Volunteerism is the fabric that makes this country go."

Many adults who get involved in Little League as parent volunteers stay on after their children are grown. Ralph Morrison began his affiliation with the George Rogers Clark Little League in Indiana back in 1961 when his son and some of his friends wanted to play baseball. Four years later, Morrison coached a team that made it to the World Series in Williamsport. And the coach had the excitement of seeing his son pitch a World Series game.

Still active in Little League as district administrator of Indiana's District 5, Morrison has managed former All-American basketball player Mike Flynn and three young men who went on to play professional baseball, including current major leaguer Walt Terrell. "Many of my former players still stay in touch with me," Morrison said. "I am proud that they remember me. That gives me just one more reason to stay involved."

Once S.W. Eighth Avenue in Fort Lauderdale, Florida, was nothing but a woody swamp. Today that site is a superb baseball complex of manicured fields. The transformation from wilderness to baseball paradise is largely the work of one man, Floyd Hull. Like many other parents, Hull became involved in Little League hoping to help provide a well-organized sports experience for his four children. Before long, the modest Florida attorney became hooked on the program. The first year he was a typical Little League father, attending the games and helping with practice sessions. In his second year he coached a team. By his third year Hull had become president of the Federal Little League, a position he continued to hold for over two decades.

More than a Little League president, Hull became a man with a mission—to convince Fort Lauderdale city officials to lease nine and a half acres of swampland to Little League so that a stadium could be constructed on that site. Years of persistence, petitions, and personal appearances before city commissioners ultimately met with success. "Little Yankee Stadium" was created, along with an impressive surrounding complex of baseball facilities.

While Hull has been singled out as the catalyst that created the complex, he has steadfastly refused to take credit for the accomplishment: "The land belongs to the city. The work has been done through donation by local citizens and fathers whose boys used the field through the years. There are hundreds of people I called at night telling them I needed them the next morning. And they

showed up. This is not just me; it's an army of people."

An associate municipal judge in Fort Lauderdale for many years, Hull continued, "I'd rather see a child out playing ball on this field than before me in court one day. The field was built for kids, and it's never locked."

The stadium has hosted the Annual Big League Baseball World Series for a number of years now, a project that requires thousands of dollars of fund-raising annually. Floyd Hull heads the fund-raising committee "because of my belief in what Little League and international competition can do for youth."

In 1979, the Freedom Foundation of Valley Forge bestowed its prestigious annual national award to the Big League world Series, "recognizing its merits to young people, to our country, and to international understanding." A year later, Floyd Hull was given the same award for a quarter-century of achievements with the Federal Little League.

For years Hull fought attempts to rename Little Yankee Stadium after him. Over his objections, the man who ranks as one of the most outstanding volunteers in the history of the Little League program re-

Russ Tinsley, three-time Emmy Award winner for sound effects, became involved in Little League when he accompanied his son, Scott, to a practice session.

ceived the recognition so many prevailed upon him to accept. Today Little League Baseball in Fort Lauderdale, Florida, is played in the Floyd Hull Stadium.

In 1950, Dominic Buonome's little son joined a Little League team in their home town of Schenectady, New York. That began Buonome's association with the program. Three years later he coached the first of three Schenectady National Little League teams to play in the World Series in Williamsport. The 1954 team won the championship.

Today Buonome is district administrator of District 12 and returns to Williamsport each August. "I stay involved," he said, "because I like the youngsters."

Three-time Emmy award winner Russ Tinsley is one of the best-known and most respected figures in the sound-editing industry. He has received Emmys for his work on *Raid on Entebbe* (1977), *Inside the Third Reich* (1982), and *The Day After* (1984). The firm he founded in 1975, Echo Film Services, has been nominated for more Emmys than any other sound-editing company in Hollywood.

Currently serving his second term as governor of the sound editor branch of the Academy of Television Arts and Sciences, Tinsley enjoys the challenge of his competitive industry. "Still, I'm thankful that the television season is over before the baseball season begins," he said. Once that time comes around, the sound editor leaves the production studio for the greener pastures of Little League playing fields, something he has been doing for over twenty years.

"I first became involved in Little League when I accompa-

One of the most important aspects of the Little League program is its family orientation—not only the volunteers but those family members who come out to cheer the teams on.

nied my son, Scott, to a practice session," Tinsley added. "He was so enthusiastic that I wanted to see what was going on. Within a year, I was president of the Tarzana Little League here in California. My boys have long since left the program, but I never have."

Together with his wife, Lee, Tinsley has continued his efforts for Little League. The pair help run the Western Regional Tournament and have made generous financial contributions to Little League projects, such as the purchase of a new scoreboard for the Western Region stadium. The talented Tinsley is also a professional photographer and has served as photographer for the Little League World Series.

"We've stayed involved," Tinsley said, "because of the special, giving people we have met through Little League. We didn't want to have known them just while our children were growing up. We want to have them in our lives forever."

In 1947, Fred Heaps began his association with Little League when his son joined the Newberry League in their home town of Williamsport, Pennsylvania, and Heaps signed on as team manager. More than twenty years later, Heaps was still managing when that Newberry team made it to the World Series. Today the indomitable Heaps is into his fourth decade of Little League management, and from all accounts shows no signs of slowing down.

Larry Dunville and Carl Cassata are two Midwesterners who between them have served as league presidents for a grand total of sixty-one years. Dunville helped found the Douglas Little League in Indianapolis, Indiana, in 1954. Cassata became president of the Harwood Heights Little League in Illinois in 1956. Both men got involved in response to their sons' desire to play Little League, yet they have retained their positions as president ever since.

Peggy Gill is a seven-year veteran in the Waldorf (Md.) American Little League who also shows no sign of letting up in her involvement. She began her volunteer efforts to share the experiences of her husband Frank (who was league president for three years) and her three sons, Michael, Christopher, and Jeffrey, who all played Little League Baseball. A certified tax accountant, Gill maintained that being her own boss has given her the flexibility she needs for Little League commitments. She has been coach, league vice president, and fund-raiser. In 1987, when the umpire-in-chief resigned, Peggy Gill stepped in and took over the role of assigning umpires for as many as twenty games per night.

"I feel the most important aspect of the Little League program is its family orientation," Gill said. "The kids learn and enjoy baseball, but it has far greater value in teaching them the necessity of teamwork and fair play."

In 1987, Peggy Gill was named Amateur Baseball Woman of the Year by the United States Baseball Federation for her varied services to Little League.

Among the thousands of outstanding volunteers who have given so much of themselves to the Little League program over the past fifty years are individuals with serious physical handicaps. Despite limitations of sight or mobility, they have worked effectively with hundreds of youngsters and provided them unforgettable examples of leadership and courage.

"The kids knew they could get away with things if they wanted to," manager Ronnie Eshelman used to say. "But I'd tell them 'I may be blind, but I'm not stupid.' " The kids on Eshelman's Allington Little League team in California during the 1970s never tried. They admired their manager, rendered sightless by a progressive disease, not only as a model of courage but for his outstanding management skills.

"I never had any difficulty with the youngsters or the parents," Eshelman said. "I probably used my ears more than the average manager. I could tell if a ball was caught by the pop of the glove. I could sense what was happening on the field by the reaction of the crowd."

Eshelman worked with each player individually, pointing out how a position should be played, hitting all the infield and outfield warm-ups. "I didn't have anything to prove," he stated. "I just enjoyed it. It was gratifying to know the boys were

Coach Ted Ferreira, who brought Little League to western Florida, was the first recepient of the Little League Baseball's President's Award.

progressing from stumbling eight-year-old kids to adroit Senior Leaguers and know I had a part in it."

Born with a birth defect that required the amputation of both legs when he was a child, Ralph Luciani never played an inning of baseball in his life. Yet as a manager in the Greater Hudson Little League in Florida in 1983 he conducted pop-up drills and hit batting practice. And Ralph Luciani did it all from the seat of a wheelchair.

"My life is working with kids. I may never get rich with money, but I'm rich with memories," said "Coach Ted" Ferreira, the first recipient of the Little League Baseball President's Award. One of the most successful high school baseball coaches in his home state of Florida for over thirty years, Ferreira is the man who was chiefly responsible for bringing Little League to Sarasota County in western Florida. "I remember our first field was carved out of a jungle of palmetto bushes," he said. Moving on to Fort Meyers, Ferreira coached Little League there for twenty-five years. The Fort Meyers playing field is named in honor of its popular coach, who had also distinguished himself as a quarterback at Auburn University in the 1940s.

Since 1977, Coach Ted has been the director of the Little League Baseball Camp in Williamsport. "Every year," Dr. Creighton Hale said, "Ted Ferreira would drive up to Williamsport from Fort Meyers in a pickup truck. After camp was over, he'd get back in his truck and head back home. He was strictly a volunteer, never receiving a cent for his services."

A few weeks before the 1987 season was set to open, Ferreira telephoned Hale with the news that his leg was going to be amputated. "I wasn't entirely surprised," Hale said, "knowing of Ted's wartime experiences. During the Second World War he had been taken prisoner by the Germans in the Battle of the Bulge. A two-day forced march to a prisoner-of-war camp in the dead of winter had resulted in his losing several toes because of frostbite. This factor and subsequent health problems that developed from his incarceration had made amputation a dreaded possibility all these years."

Hale heard from Coach Ted a few days before his operation. "Don't take my job from me, Dr. Hale," he said. "I'm going to be all right." Hale wondered how Ferreira could think of driving the two thousand miles to and from Williamsport, how he

Dr. Robert Yasui, a longtime Williamsport resident, is now in his fourth decade of service to Little League.

could think of running a summer camp program that involved eighteen hours of work a day.

"He surprised me all right," Hale said. "An amputation is a serious operation, but Ted made it back. He does the same thing on one leg that he had done so well on two."

According to Coach Ted, "I plan to stay involved until the day I die. You don't sit around just because you have a handicap. As long as I can roll out of bed in the morning, and as long as I can get to the field, I'm going to coach. Working with kids—that's my life."

Now in his fourth decade of service, Dr. Robert Yasui is one of Little League Baseball's most unusual volunteers. A longtime Williamsport resident, the physician's involvement with Little League began years before his three sons went through the Brandon League program and has continued through the decades that have followed. The fiftieth anniversary of Little League Baseball marks Dr. Yasui's thirty-fourth year as the volunteer physician on hand for the World Series in what he calls his "labor of love."

How a second-generation Japanese-American came to be a Williamsport resident and the "resident physician" for the Little League World Series is in itself a story.

Born in Hood River, Ore gon, Dr. Yasui was a student at the University of Oregon when World War II broke out. The state of war between Japan and the United States resulted in a climate of hostility and suspicion toward Japanese-Americans. "I came East," Dr. Yasui said, "to escape internment in the camps where Japanese-Americans living on the West Coast were placed. Virtually all of my family wound up detained in internment camps."

From Oregon Dr. Yasui went to Denver. From there he continued moving east until finally he settled in Philadelphia. He began medical studies at Temple University and continued at the University of Pennsylvania. An ad in a medical journal brought the young doctor to Williamsport to serve his residency in the local hospital.

"And I've been here ever since except for a time when I was in the Army," Dr. Yasui said. In 1956, his military service ended and his Little League volunteer service began. "I was always interested in sports medicine. I was already the athletic physician for the Williamsport school district and Lycoming College when I began working with the Little League World Series in 1956."

Through his more than four decades as the "World Series Doctor," Yasui has seen many changes. "The average weight of the kids has always been about a hundred five pounds, but we've had players that weighed as much as two hundred pounds and others as little as sixty or sixty-five pounds," he noted. "Today the kids

Gabby Hayes poses with members of the team he sponsored for many years.

playing in the World Series are more advanced physically than the youngsters of twenty and thirty years ago. This physical development allows for greater refinement of playing skills at an earlier age. The end result is a much higher caliber of play.

"It's evident that the Far Eastern teams have made great advances in diet and nutrition," Dr. Yasui added. "I remember very well the first team to play in the series from Japan. Those little guys averaged only ninety pounds. Then a few years ago a Korean team came in whose players were all a great deal heavier."

The Japanese-American doctor is both bemused and impressed by the good behavior of visiting Oriental youths. "The Japanese kids bow to the umpires," noted Yasui, "and the poor umpires have to bow back. The Taiwanese salute the umpires. Korean players simply give a little nod."

The doctor still chuckles at an experience he had that cut across cultural lines in a strange sort of way. "An adult member of a Japanese team became ill and was hospitalized," he recalled. "The man was complaining and trying to explain what was wrong with him. But I had never heard medical terms in Japanese. Finally, I located a Williamsport high school student who was studying Japanese. He did the translating. It turned out the man from Japan had a problem with diabetes. The whole affair was strange, to say the least: a Japanese-American doctor utilizing a Caucasian American youth to translate a Japanese adult's medical complaint. But it all worked out well for everyone in the end."

The efforts of the volunteer doctor and his volunteer staff have historically made things work out well for the Little League World Series.

"In all my years of involvement we have never had a serious injury situation develop," Yasui said. "This is credit to the great amount of attention Little League Baseball has paid to player safety. I can recall my

GABBY HAYES
BUCKEROOS

Little League would never have grown as it did without the enthusiastic support of millions of people around the world.

youthful baseball days," he continued, "when we had no helmets, no manicured fields, and equipment was in very poor condition. Today, these kids play under the safest conditions. What is more important, they have adult supervision."

Medical care is available around the clock during World Series week for, as Dr. Yasui pointed out, "the experience of participating in the World Series is too important to the children to allow even the slightest medical emergency to interrupt their fun." Assisted by his wife Phyllis, who is registered nurse, and a medical staff that knows it can call him any time of day or night, Dr. Yasui covers all the bases.

Prior to the World Series, Dr. Yasui gives each player a medical examination. "The examination is a simple screening process," he said, "to make sure no youngster has an illness or physical injury that could jeopardize participation."

As part of the volunteer army during World Series week—an army consisting of the uncles, the retirees, the people who travel hundreds of miles and give up a week's vacation to be driver of cars and vans and attend to the needs of the youngsters—the veteran doctor reflected on his impressions of World Series over the years:

"I wouldn't think of missing a World Series. It's a thrill just being involved. All the excitement and pageantry, watching kids from various parts of the world communicate through Ping Pong and pin-trading—it is always a very memorable time for me each year.

"If one could be there like I am in the dining room with the kids and see them laughing, playing, getting along with each other—it's like an international Boy Scout jamboree. And when the awards (and they're modest awards) are given out at the final dinner, it's something special. There's all that cheering for the first-place team by the teams that were defeated by them. There's no animosity, just good sportsmanship. And that's what makes the whole Little League program so worthwhile."

Coach
Chiefs
Chiefs
Chiefs

ALUMNI VOICES:

Reminiscences

Through its half-century, Little League Baseball has been a thread that sews together the lives and memories of many people. It is a common tie, a conversation-starter, a shared tapestry of experience that stretches across the years. People meet in boardrooms and offices, in schools and universities, in clubs and restaurants, on golf courses and playing fields—and the time of Little League Baseball often comes back in a rush. The Little League "alumni association" contains busdrivers and bankers, steelworkers and senators, housepainters and Hollywood stars, athletes and accountants, teachers and tax attorneys. For all of them, talking Little League Baseball is part of the fabric of their lives.

ABC-TV sportscaster **Al Trautwig** feels fortunate that his profession enables him to keep his Little League Baseball boyhood experience close to the surface. "Everyone has special feelings about his or her childhood," observed the affable commentator, "and one of the special feelings for me was Little League Baseball. It was being on a team, getting uniforms. There was never a more exciting moment than when the new uniforms came in to our league in Garden City South, New York. You'd kill to get on

Tom Selleck (third from left in back row) played for the Sherman Oaks (Ca.) Pioneer Little League team.

Today a sportscaster for ABC-TV, Al Trautwig played Little League Baseball in Garden City South, New York.

a team that had new uniforms."

Trautwig's Little League team made it "to Williamsport for weekend visitation to play some games," he recalled. "I wound up misplaying the ball in center field. It really aggravated me because it was as if I had gotten a shot to play at Shea Stadium and muffed my one big chance."

Coming full circle, or at least semicircle, Trautwig first covered the Little League World Series in Williamsport a few years ago. "I immediately went right out to center field," the ABC sportscaster noted. "Somebody hit a baseball out to me, and I caught it. That kind of made up for my muffing the ball so many years ago.

"Of all the events I've covered in my sportscasting career, the little League World Series is the one I always look forward to more than anything else. I really mean it. That's when the kids get to feel like adults, and the adults get to feel like kids."

In his work with ABC-TV, Trautwig has come into contact with many professional athletes who had played Little League, "and they all enjoy talkin' Little League Baseball. I can think of Orel Hershiser, Carney Lansford, Jim Palmer. . . . Pat McNally, the punter on the Cincinnati Bengals football team, remembers how his pants fell down once when he was playing Little League. They all have a story."

Trautwig commented, "I get a kick out of seeing the Little Leaguers emulate major leaguers. The way they dig in at the batter's box, the way they wear their glove or cap. When I played, we had guys who put sunglasses on their caps in imitation of their favorite players. And we played at night!

"For anyone who ever played Little League, that was his or her moment in the sun. He might have been pudgy, gawky, uncoordinated, shy. Most never got to the major leagues although they dreamed of doing that. But they did have Little League Baseball, and no one can ever take away those memories."

Brent Musburger of CBS-TV is one of the top sports announcers in America. His introduction to Little League Baseball came during his growing-up years in Billings, Montana. "That time was my first contact with organized sports. My father introduced Little League Baseball in Billings and also coached our championship team that first year. I played first base and batted .800. I guess that was because my mother, who was the scorekeeper, never charged anybody with an error."

The slim, intense Musburger recalled with nostalgia the summer nights under the big Montana sky playing Little League Baseball. "My father was an incredible organizer who loved kids and had a strong feeling for the values baseball could give to children," he said. "He put in countless hours teaching teams and publicizing the program. Three years after its inception, the Billings Little League program was the

One of the top sports announcers in America, CBS-TV's Brent Musburger grew up with Little League in Billings, Montana.

Former Baltimore Oriole pitcher Jim Palmer, with Dr. Creighton Hale and his stepfather, Max Palmer, who with his wife was honored in 1984 as Little League Parents of the Year.

finest in the State of Montana.

"My father took all-star teams to competitions in Oregon and California," the broadcaster recalled. "We had a lot of talent. However, we always somehow came up just a couple of runs short of reaching the big show in Williamsport."

Musburger remembered pitching in to help his father coach those Little League teams after he was no longer eligible to play himself. "We'd argue about starting lineups and baseball strategy. But, for some reason, I stayed out of any involvement in the grounds-

keeping part of the game. On the scene back then was a little nine-year-old pitcher who used to help prepare the fields for the nightly games in Billings. He had a way with a rake. That kid was a left-hander by the name of Dave McNally. Yep, the same left-hander who helped the Baltimore Orioles dominate the game in the mid-1960s and 1970s.

"So as you can see," Musburger concluded, "I'm a Little League fan. I grew up with the game. It fueled my lifelong interest in organized sports. I wouldn't trade those Little League experiences for anything."

Musburger went on from his time in Little League in Billings to excel in the world of big-time sportscasting, and the little kid who was so handy with the rake went on to excel in the world of big-time baseball. In a fourteen-year career, Dave McNally won 184 games. Four times a twenty-game winner, the crafty left-hander teamed with a stylish right-hander on the Baltimore Orioles who was also a Little League graduate.

Jim Palmer pitched for the Baltimore Orioles for nineteen years. An eight-time twenty-game winner, he was one of the best in the business.

Born in New York City in 1945, Jim was one day old when he was legally adopted by Polly and Moe Weisen. When Jim was nine years old, the family left New York and moved to California.

"I don't believe," Palmer said, "I would have ever played organized baseball had we not moved to California. Once there I didn't go to camp in the summer, so I got involved in Little League instead. I played in the Golden State Little League—all positions. I pitched, played right field, left field, whatever they wanted me to play. I was usually the best hitter and the best pitcher. I enjoyed Little League Baseball very much."

"I pitched six straight no-hitters," Palmer recalled, "and made the All-Star team. Still, our team never made the playoffs. But I had good coaches. They taught us how to play."

Just before Jim turned twelve Moe Weisen died. A while later, his mother remarried a man named Max Palmer.

"Jim and I got along good after my marriage to Polly," Max Palmer recalled. "He wanted to keep the name Weisen. And that was okay with me."

Though the adjustment to a new father-son relationship was difficult, Little League Baseball helped bring Jim and Max together. "I always took Jim to his games during his last year of Little League," Max Palmer said. "We'd play catch in the backyard. Like a lot of fathers

Nolan Ryan poses in his Little League uniform; he played in Alvin, Texas, from the age to nine to thirteen.

and sons, I still remember the closeness of those times. We really became friends."

At a postseason Beverly Hills Little League banquet two months before Christmas in the late 1950s, the league president shocked Max Palmer when he announced: "Graduating from the Yankees is James Alvin Palmer."

"What a super, super surprise that was," Max Palmer recalled. "Jim had told the league president to call him Palmer, not Weisen, but he never said anything to Polly and me. We were happily stunned. Jim changing his name to Palmer was the greatest thrill of my life. Chalk it up to Little League Baseball."

Some three decades later, Mr. and Mrs. Max Palmer were honored in 1984 in Williamsport as Little League Parents of the Year. Both father and son admitted they were "choked with emotion" on that occasion. "There still is a record of Jim Weisen in California Little League, however," the handsome pitcher-turned-broadcaster said. "One year Jim Weisen led the league in home runs, and the next year this new kid in town—Jim Palmer—ended up a good pitcher and a good hitter. But all my Little League statistics are still under the name of Weisen.

"I think back now to Little League, and I realize it gave me the first chance to play as part of a team. Most major leaguers started there. It's a very important training ground. Still that's not the reason to play Little League, obviously. The bottom line is it teaches you good values—winning is very nice, but it's not the only thing."

Today Jim Palmer, like Al Trautwig, broadcasts for ABC-TV sports, and both men have been part of the Little League Baseball World Series announcing team.

While Jim Palmer has moved from Little League to the major leagues to the broadcasting booth, a contemporary of his still plies his trade on the pitcher's mound. **Nolan Ryan** is the greatest strikeout pitcher in the history of baseball. His fastball has been timed at over a hundred miles an hour. He is the only man in history to pitch five no-hitters. And he, like Palmer, began his organized sports activity in Little League.

"The first Little League field in Alvin, Texas, where I grew up," Ryan recalled, "was cleared by my dad and the fathers of the other kids in the program. My brother Robert played on that field, but by the time I came along, we had a different one. I played Little League from the time I was nine years old until I was thirteen. Some of my fondest memories of baseball come from those years.

"Just making the Little

League team was a thrill for all of us in Alvin. When we'd get our caps and uniforms, we'd be so proud, we'd wear those caps to school. The uniforms were made of heavy flannel," the well-built, soft-spoken Ryan continued, "and we played in the Texas heat. But no one seemed to pay the weather any heed."

Now in his third decade of major league pitching, the Texas Rangers fireballer recalled how he and his friends fantasized about playing in the World Series in Williamsport. "We never won a championship," Ryan said. "But we tried real hard. I guess that's what Little League is all about—trying."

Today the holder of nearly forty pitching records, Ryan still vividly recalls a moment during a Little League ceremony when a guest speaker told the members of his team that one day one of them would go on to play in the major leagues. "When I heard what he said, it was like a bell went off in my head," Ryan said. "I became very excited. When I got home, I told my mom about the ceremony and what the man said.

" 'Mom,' I said, 'that man was talking about me.'

" 'What do you mean?' she asked.

" 'It's me that he meant, Mom. I'm sure it was me he was talking about.'

"I remember that experience as vividly as if it happened yesterday—the sun, the standing in the field, the man's voice, his words. I never forgot it."

In 1987, Nolan Ryan's mother, Martha Lee Ryan, and late father, Lynn Nolan, Sr., were honored as Little League Parents of the Year in Williamsport. Whether Mrs. Ryan remembered that long-ago scene in Alvin, Texas, and her son's sense of his future no one knows. But both Martha Lee Ryan and Nolan Ryan admitted to a great deal of satisfaction in his career and her being so honored.

Little League continues to be part of Nolan Ryan's life. His wife Ruth coached their son Reid in Little League for one year and their son Reese and daughter Wendy in the Minor League Division. Ryan admitted to a poignancy in the fact his children have played and continue to play Little League in the same small Texas town and on the same field on which he once played.

Ryan has contributed support to the Little League Texas State Center in Waco. The Nolan Ryan Little League Baseball Summer Camp Scholarship was established by the pitcher to provide an opportunity for a Texas youngster to attend camp at Waco. At home in Alvin, Little League youngsters hold practice sessions on a ballfield on the Ryan property.

For all the Ryans, the full sweep of their Little League experience represents a sense of community and continuity. It is also, as Reid Ryan put it, "a lot of fun with all the parents getting into it and sometimes as many as two hundred people at a game."

After three generations of involvement in Little League Nolan Ryan reflected, "The program has always been a big part of our family, and I hope it always will be."

Throughout the years, power-pitcher Nolan Ryan, until recently with the Houston Astros, throwing to power-hitter **Mike Schmidt** of the Philadelphia Phillies had been one of the classic confrontations in major league baseball. Both men are virtually assured of entering Baseball's Hall of Fame, and both got their start in baseball in Little League. But where Ryan admitted "I was a good player, not a great player as a Little Leaguer," Schmidt was a baseball prodigy.

In the North Riverdale, Ohio, league the little freckle-faced, rusty-haired Mike Schmidt entered at the age of nine, his talents were immediately recognized. His ability was

Today the holder of nearly forty pitching records, Nolan Ryan remembers how he and his friends fantasized about playing in the World Series in Williamsport.

so outstanding that the youngster was at once drafted into the major league division for eleven-to-twelve-year-olds.

Jack Fenner, a coach and founder of the North Riverdale league, had heard reports of Schmidt's prodigious talents before he actually saw him play. "We were having tryouts for the 1958 season for boys twelve and under in one place, and boys ten and under in another," Fenner said. "They were doing certain drills. I didn't know who Schmidt was, but in the younger group, I saw this little kid with a terrific arm. He was catching the ball behind his back. I said to myself, 'That has to be Schmidt. And I must draft him.' Mike was my number-one pick and the third kid picked overall in the draft, and he was only nine years old."

Schmidt likewise was on the lookout for Mr. Fenner. "I had heard he was a strict disciplinarian, a tough guy. When I got on his team, I was at the age when I should have been playing T-ball," Schmidt recalled, "and I have to admit I was a little bit in awe of him. But things worked out fine.

"Mr. Fenner was my first baseball coach, and I can't say enough about what he did for me," Schmidt continued. "I learned a lot from him. There were some humorous moments too. I still remember his bunt signal. If his pipe was upside down, that meant we should bunt. One day, there was a little light mist, and Mr. Fenner turned his pipe upside down to keep the rain out. About six guys in a row bunted."

Mike Schmidt played Little League Baseball in North Riverdale, Ohio.

Today Mike Schmidt, power hitter for the Philadelphia Phillies, is virtually assured entry into Baseball's Hall of Fame.

With Schmidt in his lineup, Jack Fenner won four North Riverdale Little League championships in five years. Fenner's teams lost only four times in sixty games over a five-year period. During that time, Schmidt played shortstop and third base as well as caught and pitched. When he was ten years old, in his second year of Little League, the highly competitive redheaded boy who seemingly always wore his baseball uniform pitched three no-hitters, turned a triple play at third base, and batted .737. Once he struck out seventeen of the eighteen batters he faced. When he was twelve he slammed eighteen home runs in a dozen games and was featured in stories in Dayton, Ohio, newspapers.

"I had plenty of thrills playing Little League," Schmidt recalled, "no doubt about that. One that stands out in my mind is the time our team went to the district semi-finals. I was pitching. I pitched a no-hitter and lost. Yes, lost! I was eleven years old. My best friend, Jeff

Allen, pitched against me. He pitched a one-hitter and won. And he scored the game's only run. He got on base. I can't exactly remember how, but he got on. He stole second. I tried to pick him off and overthrew the ball. He finally scored. I was quite embarrassed.

"Little League was where I learned for the first time the seriousness of team competition," Schmidt said. "It was the first time I got to wear a team uniform with team colors. My grandmother was the one who usually put me in my uniform because my parents worked in the summer, and she took care of me. She would have that uniform ironed and spotless; I remember it was white with green stripes and green letters. There was a green hat, and little rubber spikes, and baseball socks and all that. I couldn't wait to get that uniform on and get driven to the ballpark and do all that business."

One of the great sluggers in major league history, Schmidt maintained, "Whenever I'm

From left to right, Dr. Creighton Hale, Mr. and Mrs. Jack Schmidt, and Mike Schmidt, as the Schmidts are honored as Parents of the Year in 1981.

asked how I got my start in baseball, I always answer with great pride that it was Little League. The dedication and desire I have as a major leaguer was put into me by Little League. There are kids all around the country, all around the world getting that same chance I got. And that's because of the adults who are involved. I can't praise them enough. They give their time and their effort to develop the skills of the young players."

Schmidt's parents never coached or managed but were nevertheless actively involved in Little League. "We were happy just to be sponsors and fans," said Joseph Schmidt, Mike's father. "Mike played on the team sponsored by our family company. We never missed a game in which he played. What my wife, Lois, and I liked to do was sit in the stands and watch the games.

"We still are friends with people we met in Little League when Mike was playing," Lois Schmidt added. "They are mothers and fathers who have worked in the concession stands, managed, umpired, been league officers."

Mike Schmidt's parents were honored as Little League Parents of the Year in 1981.

The Little League Parents of the Year Award has been presented annually since 1981. The award recognizes the role played by parents in the Little League program and specifically designates the parents of a major leaguer who were actively involved in their child's Little League experiences. On August 23, 1985, the award was presented to Jim Carter, father of **Gary Carter** of the New York Mets.

Gary Carter played in the West Fullerton Little League in California. His father coached his team. "My dad," Carter recalled, "was not only my coachbut my best friend while I was growing up. My mom passed away when I was eleven years old, and Little League proved to be the saving grace in my life at the time.

New York Mets catcher Gary Carter played in the West Fullerton Little League in California.

Jim Carter, with his son Gary (left) and Dr. Creighton Hale (right) receives his trophy as 1985 Little League Parent of the Year.

"My dad and I became very close after Mom's passing, and much of our time was spent on the Little League field. Dad would pitch to me, hit out fly balls, give me tips on how to take care of my glove. We'd spend many hours just talking baseball. That time added so much to my development not only as a player, but also as a person. I can still recite the Little League pledge today. It says win or lose, always do your best. I took those words to heart. That's what I learned most from Little League Baseball."

The amiable Met catcher continued: "The Little League program is a kind of farm system where players have the opportunity of proving themselves. Scouts come around to watch the kids and look at their development. If a kid improves consistently and stays with the game, he can wind up becoming a major leaguer from that start in Little League."

Carter has felt the need to give back to Little League. He has performed an introduction to a film on safety and a television public service announcement on Little League. "I've donated all my Little League trophies to the museum at Williamsport," Carter noted, "as well as one of the first gloves I ever used. I did keep one thing, however, an All-Star hat with a lot of buttons and pins on it. That I'm saving for my son."

Dale Murphy of the Atlanta Braves is a Gold Glove Award center fielder, a two-time National League Most Valuable Player, and one of the classiest athletes in all of sports. He played in the Tualatin Little League in Portland, Oregon. And his parent were also honored as Little League Parents of the Year receiving the award in 1986.

Charles Murphy coached his son in the minor leagues. "I remember Dale getting his first uniform and trying to put it on," he recalled. "The socks were especially difficult, and his mother had to help him with them."

"I remember how excited I was the day we were scheduled to play our first game under the lights," the Atlanta slugger said. "It was a great feeling thinking we would be on the field just like the major leaguers. I was only nine years old.

"That first season," Murphy smiled in recollection, "I had only one hit. Fortunately my parents didn't let me know that wasn't very good."

"When Dale entered the next level of the program,"

Atlanta Braves center fielder Dale Murphy played in the Tualatin Little League in Portland, Oregon.

Charles Murphy said, "I stepped aside. There was no reason for me to continue as a coach on Dale's team. The men who directed his team at the major league level of Little League had the kids' best interests at heart, and they knew their baseball. I couldn't have asked for more."

Dale Murphy agreed. "My coaches were good people who taught us the essential skills necessary to play the game. They taught us to compete but didn't overemphasize winning. They instilled in me a good feeling for baseball," Murphy added. "Because of that feeling, I wanted to pursue baseball as a career simply because it was so much fun. I give Little League credit for making this game fun.

"My main goal for the rest of my career," the 6-foot-6 power hitter said, "is really not to win a third MVP award. I would like to win a World Series, but I will be satisfied if I can just go out every day and enjoy playing the game. It has to be fun like Little League."

When Joe and Millie Garvey received the Little League Parent of the Year Award in 1982, Mr. Garvey recalled the time he first noticed his son's major league potential. "When Steve was eleven," Joe Garvey said, "and playing for the Drew Park Cardinals in a Little League in Tampa, Florida, he was also working out each spring with the Dodgers. That was because I drove the bus for the Dodgers when they came from Vero Beach to the west coast of Florida to play spring exhibition games. I would bring little Steve along with me.

"One day he was standing next to a coach," Garvey added, "who was tapping ground balls to infielders. Steve would catch the ball when it was thrown to a coach, then flip the ball to the coach. One infielder forgot that the person catching the throws was just a kid. He whirled and threw the ball as hard as he could from only forty feet away.

"Steve stood his ground and caught the ball. Most kids would have ducked. And even though his hand was swollen and sore, Steve tried to look nonchalant as he flipped the ball to the coach. Later, one of the Dodgers said to me, 'That kid is not afraid of the ball. He's a natural ballplayer.'

"And I thought to myself, 'Hey, maybe someday Steve can be a big leaguer.' But I never dreamed he'd wind up playing for the same team that I drove around in my Greyhound bus."

For **Steve Garvey**, who went on to become an All-Star first baseman and one of the most popular players in the history of the Los Angeles Dodgers, Little League has left some indelible memories. "There were the embarrassing moments

Steve Garvey played Little League Baseball for the Drew Park Cardinals in Tampa, Florida.

Steve Garvey, Joe (his father), Dr. Creighton Hale, Millie (Steve's mother), and a representative of Woman's Day *at the ceremonies honoring the Garveys as 1982 Parents of the Year.*

in Little League when I played shortstop," the handsome Garvey recalled. "I made a lot of errors. Some balls went right between my legs.

"And there were the unforgettable challenges. Once in a while I'd pitch. I remember a tournament game we were in that went nine innings. I pitched all nine and struck out twenty, allowing just one hit. And we lost the game.

"That was the first time I ever extended myself physically. I was twelve years old. I came to realize that was good for me. And I carried that experience over to the major leagues.

"But probably what I remember most over the long run from Little League," Garvey said," are the friendships with other boys that have lasted over the years. Long after you forget the scores or how you won or lost, you still remember the people."

In 1988 the mother and father of Los Angeles Dodgers pitcher **Orel Hershiser** were honored as the Little League Parents of the Year. "The award is not something I earned for them by being a major league pitcher," Hershiser said. "It's something they earned a long time ago because of the effort they put into my brothers and me."

That effort was a family affair. Hershiser's father functioned as manager, coach, umpire, groundskeeper, and district administrator in the Southfield Little League outside of Detroit, Michigan, where Orel grew up. His mother worked in the concession stands.

"The whole family's heartbeat was around Little League Baseball," Hershiser recalled. "Even though my dad was traveling a lot, he always managed to be there at the games. I can remember him coming home from the airport, taking off his tie and jacket, and getting out onto the field and into the swing of things."

Hershiser's brothers Judd and Gordie also played Little League Baseball. "With three

LEFT: *Los Angeles Dodgers pitcher Orel Hershiser (right) with his parents as they are honored as Little League Parents of the Year in 1988.*

RIGHT: *As a twelve-year-old, Orel Hershiser was the Most Valuable Player on his Little League team outside Detroit, Michigan.*

kids involved plus my parents, we were hardly ever around at the dinner table at the same time. Somebody either had the early game and was out playing while the kid with the later game might be home eating. My mom might be working the concession stand for the early game and my dad might be getting ready to ump the later game. Most of the time we had picnic lunches that my mom made, and we ate right at the facility."

For Orel Hershiser, like so many others, Little League Baseball was the first organized sports experience. The Indians, one of the Little League teams he played for, has a special significance for the Dodger pitcher, because it was a team with a lot of history and prestige.

"It was an honor to be a member of the Indians, a team managed by a man named Mike Griffith," Hershiser recalled. "Mr. Griffith had preseason and in-season dinners for his team. He talked a lot about all of us having pride in what we did. It was exciting to play for him. I pitched, played shortstop, second base. I played wherever they needed me."

It was while playing Little League that Hershiser first discovered that he needed glasses. "I was hitting .600 or something like that my first year, and then in the second half of the season my average dropped to .200 or so. I got my eyes checked out, got glasses, and my average started to go back up again."

The right-handed hurler acknowledged that through his early years in Little League he was not the best player on his teams. "I had to keep working hard at it, constantly trying to improve," he said. "I still recall those days of driving home in the car from games with my dad. We used to get a large soda if we won and a small one if we lost. I have to admit that I hated to lose."

As a twelve-year-old Hershiser was the Most Valuable Player on his Little League team. He has a vivid memory of that time. "We were in the district tournament. It was the sixth inning, and I knew this would be my last game in Little League because we were losing by about three or four runs. I came up to bat. There were two outs and nobody on. I remember thinking that this was going to be my last at-bat in Little League so I want to make it count. I wanted to hit a home run. On the second pitch I did hit a home run. Rounding the bases, I thought well at least this is the way to go out!"

Today one of major league baseball's most effective pitchers, Hershiser likes to joke: "I was very successful in Little League. From there my career

Little League was a family affair for Orel Hershiser. His father functioned as manager, coach, umpire, groundskeeper, and district administrator, while his mother worked in the concession stand.

went downhill. I got cut from my high school and college teams in my freshman and sophomore years. I was drafted by the Dodgers in the seventeenth round. I spent four and a half years in the minor leagues. I always dreamed of making it in the big leagues but for a time there it looked like it would never happen for me. I just worked and never let myself or anyone else think that my dream wouldn't come true.

"There's a real parallel between my Little League experience and my professional career: participate, get cut, learn how to make the team, work, perform, and excel. That's been the formula.

"Today with the Los Angeles Dodgers, I just go out there and try to do my best every day. It's like I'm living out the dream of a kid who was funny-looking, wore glasses, and had arms down to his knees who ended up playing in the majors."

Mel Stottlemeyer is today the highly successful pitching coach of the New York Mets. He was a star pitcher for the New York Yankees. But his baseball roots are in Little League.

"I've been involved in Little League in a lot of different ways," Stottlemeyer said. "I played it as a youngster in Williston, South Carolina. I don't remember how well I did, but I do remember I welcomed the opportunity to play in a good program. It gave me a starting point in baseball.

"Both my boys—Todd, who is today a member of the Toronto Blue Jays, and Mel, Jr., who is in the high minor leagues—were Little Leaguers, and I got involved as a coach. One summer I had to go on a business trip. Our team was undefeated at the time. I left the team in the charge of my wife, who was a nervous wreck until I returned. She didn't take any chances losing a game. She pitched one of my boys and the other one caught. And if there was any relief pitching to do—one of those boys would relieve the other. We've always been a Little League family.

"I own a sporting goods store in Washington, and we're sponsors of a Little League team there," the student of pitching added. "My partner has spent a number of years as president of the league. If I weren't so involved with the New York Mets today, I would still go out and watch a game now and then and enjoy the way Little Leaguers play."

One of the most exciting players to arrive in the major leagues in a long time is the St. Louis Cardinal left fielder **Vince Coleman**. This mercurial outfielder, still at the beginning of his career, is already one of baseball's best when it comes to base-stealing. He began stealing bases when he played Little League Baseball in Jacksonville, Florida.

"I always looked forward to playing those Little League games. When I was growing up and watching baseball on TV, hustling Pete Rose and the Big Red Machine appealed to me. I would go out and try to be like Pete Rose and the other players on Cincinnati whenever Saturday night rolled around and I got my chance to play.

"My first team was the Scottsboro Cubs. My manager, Mr. Pearson, is still clear in my memory," Coleman recalled. "He gave me a chance to play. He and all my other managers deserve a lot of credit. They took the time to work with me, they put up with me, and they had the patience.

"I played second base and was the pitcher," the speedy outfielder added. "At that time, the sign of playing well was getting dirty. If you didn't get dirty, you weren't playing a good game. But if you did, everybody knew you were on base. So when you got a double or something, you'd be sure to slide in to the base. All the players were good runners and tried to steal. But," Coleman smiled, "stealing was already a forte of mine.

"We kids in Jacksonville were just pleased as could be to go out and play every Saturday. We didn't look for much more than that. Little League was the first organized sport I participated in. They gave us schedules, uniforms. We had a manager, umpires, a neat field that was marked off every Saturday. After the game, we looked forward to buying a soda and a package of potato chips. That's the way it was," Coleman said, "we had all the good things to look forward to and we really enjoyed those Little League times."

Tom Brunansky was born in West Covina, California. In 1988 he was traded by the Minnesota Twins to the St. Louis Cardinals and became an outfield teammate of Vince Coleman. Brunansky has his own special memories of Little League:

"What comes to mind when I think of Little League," he said, "are uniforms that never fit me. I was always one of the biggest kids, and there always seemed to be a panic of people rushing around trying to find a uniform big enough to fit. Come picture day, I always had a problem.

"Little League," the man they call "Bruno" added, "was a big influence in my becoming a major leaguer. I remember watching my brother play Little League, and boy, I could hardly wait to play. When I finally got to begin playing at the age of eight, we didn't have T-ball. We'd go out there and hit against real pitchers. We had some pretty long games, and some pretty high scores. A final tally of twenty-six to twenty-two was typical."

Pitchers **Tommy John** and **Don Sutton** are now in their third decade of pitching in the major leagues. Their Little League Baseball days are far behind them, yet both veteran pitchers still have vivid memories of those times.

John, like so many other Little Leaguers, was managed by his father. "I thought the way he handled all of us boys in Terre Haute, Indiana, was just the greatest," the former New York Yankee pitcher noted. "Dad had us practicing two and three times a week. He was a stickler on fundamentals, always managed to have a kind word for all the kids, and gave all of us a chance to play.

"The thing that really stands out in my mind," continued John, "was how he impressed on us that it was fun to do things the right way. One of his 'purpose' drills was to lay shinguards on the infield about ten feet up each base line. We would then take turns practicing bunting at those shinguards. Any time a bunter would manage to hit one of those shinguards, there would be a

"We had a lot of fun playing Little League ball. Our only disappointment was that we never won a spot in the World Series," recalls pitcher Tommy John.

Pitcher Don Sutton remembers his Little League coach, Henry Roper, as a major influence on his career in baseball.

reward—an ice cream cone. Dad wound up treating quite of few of the kids to ice cream cones."

The bunting practice and all the other drills paid off; John's Little League team, in his phrase, "swept everything in town." That caused some problems for the dry cleaning business that sponsored the team.

"Since we did so well, we were our own kind of mini-dynasty. Our sponsor got so much flak that he finally gave up his affiliation with the team. But we had no trouble getting a new sponsor—Green Line Trucking. And we kept on winning. We had seasons like twenty to nothing, eighteen to two, nineteen to one.

"I pitched some, won quite a few games, and played first base when I wasn't pitching," the laid-back, softspoken John said. "We had a lot of fun playing Little League ball. Our only disappointment was that we never won a spot in the World Series."

John finally made it to Williamsport in 1962 when, as a young pitcher in the minors' Eastern League, he conducted a clinic for the Brandon Little League. "I really enjoyed doing that," John said. "It was like going back to the beginning of Little League. The Brandon League, founded in 1946, was one of the very first."

Don Sutton was born in Clio, Alabama, and began what he called "my organized baseball career" in Cantonment, Florida. It was there that the lively Sutton started out at age eleven as a shortstop in Little League. One year later he became a pitcher.

"When I was twelve years old," Sutton said, "we got a new sixth-grade teacher named Henry Roper. He was also going to be our Little League coach when the season began. I learned that he had once pitched in the minor leagues so I stuck to him all winter like a flea stays with a dog.

"We became close. And he's the one who really taught me how to pitch." Roper must have taught Sutton well. "I was nine to zero," the well-traveled Sutton recalled, "with three no-hitters and a perfect game. I got my name in the paper. All of that was the biggest thrill of my life."

Henry Roper, the Little League Baseball coach who had such an impact on Don Sutton's life, has since passed away. "I miss him," Sutton admitted. "I would often call him after big games. Sometimes I would call him for advice. He always said that one of his biggest thrills was seeing a kid he coached pitch in the 1977 All-Star Game."

Sutton acknowledged, "I'd like to coach kids myself someday. I think that would be a way to repay Henry Roper for what he did for me. If I could do something that would give one child a chance to come as far as I have come, then I'd feel maybe Henry Roper would be paid back."

The man they called **"Bullet Bob" Turley** was just concluding his professional pitching career when Tommy John and Don Sutton came onto the major league scene. Turley, who won 101 games in a career that spanned the years 1951 to 1963, admitted, "If it hadn't been for Little League, I would not have made the major leagues. Until Little League arrived in East St. Louis, Illinois, we played Indian ball. That was a game where you had only two or three players," Turley said. "One kid pitched underhanded to a batter who tried to hit the ball as far as he could. That was the only baseball I knew then.

"In the summer of 1943 I was twelve years old, and Little League came to town. It was in the middle of World War II and many of the fathers were overseas—so, in a way, having Little League gave all of us a chance to be watched after by kind of surrogate fathers. For us kids, the equipment seemed about the most important thing. We had brand-new bats, shiny baseballs, and something we found impossible to believe—uniforms, real uniforms!

"I never cared much about baseball until the league started. Then suddenly I was in love with it enough to make it a career."

Ron Santo was a slugging third baseman for the Chicago Cubs in the 1960s and 1970s. As a youngster he played Little League in his home state of Washington. In 1966 Santo owned a pizzeria that sponsored a team in Park Ridge, Illinois. "I felt like I was giving back to Little League by sponsoring a team," he said. "We'd win some, and we'd lose some. Sometimes we'd even cry. But then we'd get together and have a pizza and get ready for the next game."

Tim Teufel arrived in the majors in 1983 with the Minnesota Twins. Today the versatile infielder is a member of the New York Mets.

"I started playing Little League Baseball in Greenwich, Connecticut, when I was eight years old," he recalled. "What I remember is the organization and the discipline that it gave us for every aspect of life, not only baseball. We were on a schedule—practice at three o'clock meant I was there at three. Little League got us organized early on in life and that was good. It put a time frame on everything, be it a five-o'clock game or three-o'clock practice. We all learned a sense of responsibility.

"In Greenwich, we won our town championship three years in a row; we had a darn good team. My dad was our coach. We practiced three days a week, played baseball five days a week.

"When we played it was a gathering of the community. Everybody knew each other. The kids all grew up in the area, played with each other," Teufel said, "the parents knew each other. The community aspect of the game was strong.

"I was mainly a pitcher and shortstop. I was a good pitcher with one of the first curve balls in the league where I was able to swing it and break it about two feet. That was big.

"You've got to start somewhere, the earlier the better. Little League gave me that—the organization, the rules, the fundamentals."

First baseman and catcher on the St. Louis Cardinals, **Tom Pagnozzi** played Little League in Tucson, Arizona. "My memories are very good," Pagnozzi recalled. "We went to the Washington regionals when I was in the eleven- to twelve-year-old division. It was really something traveling as a group. The year before our league went to the World Series and was defeated by Taiwan, so we were the defending national champion. It was really big, a lot of fun, playing in the Washington regional before almost twelve thousand people when you're eleven years old. That's something I'll never forget.

"Ever since Little League, I knew I wanted to become a major league ball player," said Pagnozzi. "With the success I had at an early age, I was prepared for what came later on. I was a pitcher and played short. My father was umpire-in-chief; he controlled umpiring for the whole league from T-ball to seniors. He had to make sure there were umpires at four divisions, eight games a day. At one time he was president of the league. I came from a strong baseball background. I had two brothers who played professional baseball. They never got to the majors, but Little League Baseball was everything to us."

New York Mets utility player Lee Mazzilli played in the South Highway Little League in Brooklyn, New York.

Lee Mazzilli, who was born in Brooklyn, New York, in 1955, has been a major leaguer since 1976. He began his career as an exciting young ballplayer with the New York Mets, played for the Pittsburgh Pirates, and now, having come full circle, is back in New York winding down his tenure in the majors as a Mets utility player.

"I began playing baseball in Little League," the veteran first baseman said. "I played in the South Highway Little League in Brooklyn, which today is named after Gil Hodges. I played center field and was a pretty good fielder. Before Little League, all I knew was schoolyard baseball or baseball on the concrete streets of Brooklyn. So playing on a field with grass and dirt was a really nice experience. It was just like baseball on TV. I still remember how much we enjoyed wearing the uniforms and having such good playing conditions. I still say it was the most exciting part of my life as a youngster. Every time I ran out on the field, it was a thrill.

"My favorite player during my Little League years was Willie Mays," Mazzilli laughed, "me and about a million other kids. We did well in Little League, won a couple of championships. Still I think the question of winning at that level wasn't as important as having fun and enjoying the game. Little League gave me that feeling of enjoyment."

Roy White was born on December 27, 1943, in Los Angeles. From 1965 to 1979 he played in almost two thousand games for the New York Yankees. But before that there was Little League.

I played "Little League in Compton, California," White said, "and that time was my first experience with organized baseball.

"What was pretty impressive about the Compton West Little League that I played in was that three or four players from that league went on to play major league ball. Right offhand I can name you Reggie Smith, who played with the Red Sox, Cardinals, and Dodgers; Don Wilson, who pitched for the Houston Astros; Lenny Randall, who played in the majors. All of us played together in Compton West Little League. It was always a hot baseball area.

"I think we had coaches who were interested in kids and wanted to teach us the right way to play baseball," White recalled. "I think we did receive pretty good coaching for that level. Our team only managed to get as far as the first round for the World Series. We all kind of dreamed about playing in the World Series in Williamsport, but unfortunately our team was not good enough.

"My son played Little League, three, four years ago and right now I'm teaching hitting at an indoor facility to eight- to ten-year-olds who are playing Little League, so in a way I still have an involvement in Little League."

"I was taught things at the age of ten that some guys don't know when they're in the minors," says Eddie Murray about his Little League years.

Eddie Murray, a star for years of the Baltimore Orioles, is a latter-day graduate of the Compton, California, Little League that spawned White and so many other fine athletes. "I was in the Compton American Little League," Murray recalled. "And my teammates and I were very lucky kids. We had a super coach. You wouldn't believe the fundamentals we learned. I was taught things at the age of ten that some guys don't know when they're in the minors."

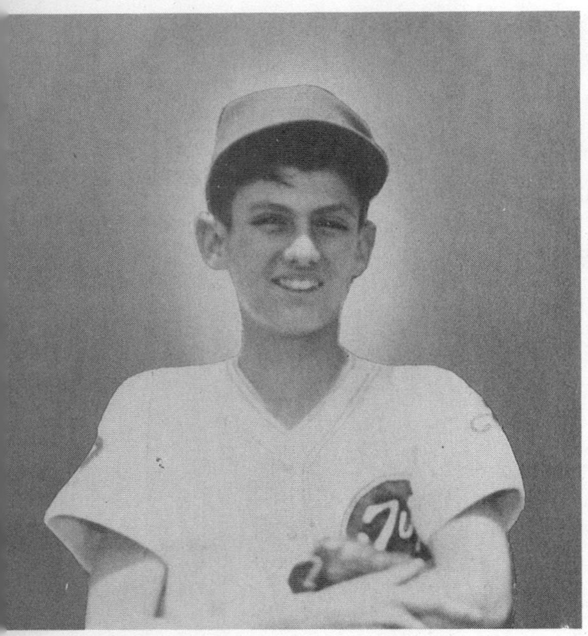

Rollie Fingers is another graduate of the California Little League.

Rollie Fingers is another Californian who distinguished himself in Little League and the major leagues. In 1981 the mustached Fingers, pitching for the Milwaukee Brewers, won the American League's Cy Young Award and also the Most Valuable Player Award. It was a big league first. He was also the first relief pitcher to win the American League's MVP award.

"I won a lot of awards in the majors," Fingers said, "but none of them was as exciting as my making the Citrus League All-Star Team when I played Little League Baseball in Cucamonga, California. That's probably because it came to me at such a young age. As a boy, I felt that was the most thrilling thing that could ever happen to me. And probably it was.

"Pitching in Little League was always exciting," Fingers continued, "maybe as exciting as it was pitching in my first of three World Series in 1972 for Oakland."

Davey Lopes had a long major league career playing for such teams as the Los Angeles Dodgers and the Houston Astros. But his highlight memories of Little League span some twenty-three years. In 1959 he played on a championship team in Providence, Rhode Island. "I'll never forget that time from my boyhood and the manager of my Little League team, Amos Ventor," Lopes said. "He was like a father to me."

In 1981, Lopes was the color commentator for the television broadcast of the Little League World Series. "Tai-chung, Taiwan, edged Tampa four to two in the title game," he recalled. "Being there rekindled all my fond memories of Little League and the time I played in Rhode Island."

Davey Lopes was the color commentator for the television broadcast of the Little League World Series in 1981.

"When I was growing up in Long Beach, California," recalled San Diego Padre outfielder **Tony Gwynn**, "my idol was Willie Davis of the Dodgers. His number was three. When they handed out the Little League uniform numbers that went from one to fifteen, I tried like heck to get number three but I couldn't. That was because the guys on the team who were there from the year before got to pick the numbers they wanted. I had to settle for number eleven."

That was the only disappointing experience in Little League Baseball for the left-handed-hitting Gwynn. "I still remember those days," he said, "playing for the Long Beach Hornets in the Kiwanis League. My manager was Dick Ortega, and he was helped out by his brother Al. It was the first time I played organized anything. Everybody on the team had a chance to play. I played first base and center field. And although I never started and only played the last three innings, Little League was always a lot of fun."

The two-time National League batting champion recalled sitting at home on Wednesday nights "waiting for my older brother Charles to come back from Little League and wondering whether his team had won or lost. Charles was the first in Little League, then I and then my brother Chris followed. My dad helped out as a driver. Later when I moved up he became an umpire."

The personable Gwynn admitted that he was just an average player in Little League and that he never dreamed he would become one of major league baseball's best hitters. "But I did realize that Little League Baseball taught me some important lessons at an early age. It organized me. Baseball is a team game played by individuals. I learned through Little League that you sometimes have to give yourself up as a hitter to move the runner along. For a kid sacrificing yourself for the good of the team is not always what you want to do. But it was an important lesson for me, for any kid to learn about baseball."

Now twenty-eight years old and one of baseball's most respected hitters, Gwynn recalled a moment in Little League, in his words, "as if it happened yesterday, my best, my fondest memory of that time.

"It was the championship game of the Kiwanis League. Both teams were undefeated and there was a lot of talking from people on both sides about who was going to win. We played a tough game for five innings. Then in the sixth inning, the last inning of that game, we just blew them out. It seemed like everybody on my team got a hit or scored a run. After the last out was made, everybody ran out to the pitcher's mound and started jumping on top of each other just like the professionals. We sprayed soda on each other just like it was the World Series.

"I played at other levels, and we won other championships. But that first one meant so much to me and to all the others . . . a bunch of ten- and eleven-year-old kids just having a great time."

Mike Greenwell of the Boston Red Sox was born in Louisville, Kentucky, and moved to Florida with his family when he was five years old. Two years later Greenwell took part in his first organized sports experience with the Mets in the North Fort Meyers (Fla.) Little League.

"I was always one of the smallest guys back then," says the Boston slugger. "I batted first or second in the batting order. But from day one in Little League Baseball, I felt I would play in the major leagues one day. I was a pitcher in Little League, but I pitched just so I could get them out and get up to hit. I had a very good fastball and could bring it, as they say. My biggest moment in Little League was striking out my hundred-fifty-fifth batter—still the all-time season record for the North Fort Meyers Little League."

Pointing out that his parents never missed a game he played in, Greenwell admits that Little League "made me love baseball. Today I'm still involved with the program. I run a baseball clinic in Fort Meyers every year for the Little League kids. It's nice to give something back."

Looking back at his Little League days, Greenwell takes satisfaction in the fact that he's "no longer one of the little guys. Now I'm the number-four hitter, a power hitter on the Boston Red Sox, not the number-one or number-two hitter the way I had been in Little League. No one ever thought I'd hit home runs back then. Still I was always able to put the ball in the play."

Among the things that helped Greenwell "put the ball in play" were those endless afternoons in Fort Meyers watching the Kansas City Royals and his boyhoood idol **George Brett** go through their spring training routines. "I used to watch Brett and look in the mirror, wanting to look like him. Now if you look at the way George Brett swings and the way I do—you'll see a lot of George Brett in my swing."

A decade before Mike Greenwell put on his Little League uniform, George Brett was a catcher playing for the Tigers in the El Segundo Little

League in California. El Segundo was a small city with a population of only 14,000 back then, but it was nevertheless a big baseball community.

"We had six or eight Little League teams," says Brett "and kids were out there playing three hundred sixty-five days a year. I followed my three brothers into the program," the Kansas City Royals star points out. "We were all two years apart, and my parents spent a lot of time involved with Little League with the four of us playing at one time or another."

The memory of getting three stitches in his mouth when a "kid came home and into me and didn't slide," the excitement of being a twelve-year-old on an All-Star team that "went further than any other team in the history of El Segundo—we won the area, the region, the section, and got those little pins to put our caps," the thrill of "having my first organized sports experience with coaching, uniforms, and all of that" are all things George Brett remembers well.

But what he remembers best is the fun and the impact Little League Baseball had on him. "The thing I try to do playing baseball in the major leagues is have fun," says the affable hitter. "When you play Little League Baseball it's fun, not a job. You go out there with your buddies and play baseball. That's what I do now in the majors. I don't think of playing baseball as a job. I think of it as playing and having fun.

"As crazy as it seems," adds Brett, "I still remember the Little League Pledge: 'I trust in God. I love my country and respect its laws. I will play fair and strive to win. But win or lose I will always do my best.' That," Brett emphasizes, "is pretty much what major league baseball is all about too."

In the connection between Little League and the major leagues is a clear link between boyhood dreams and adult realization. Yet there are those who have achieved fame in other walks of life who still retain vivid memories of playing Little League Baseball.

Kansas City Royals infielder George Brett played catcher for the Tigers in the El Segundo Little League in California.

Turk Schonert is one of them. Best known for his quarterback play in the National Football League, Schonert is also remembered for his Little League play as a third baseman for the Bolsa team of Garden Grove, California, that represented the United States West in the 1968 Little League World Series.

"My most striking memory," Schonert recalled, "is being told we were going to fly somewhere to play baseball. That was a big deal. We thought we were just like the pros. Once we got to Williamsport, we felt like we really accomplished something as a team. We made friends with kids on all the teams. We played Japan, and they won. But the outcome of the games didn't really matter much. All of us kids had become friends from spending the week together in the camp, and the friendships were the important things. They are what I remember most."

Today **Mike Ditka** is the highly respected coach of the Chicago Bears in the National Football League. When he was eleven years old, he was a highly competitive catcher for the Little League team sponsored by Plodnick's Furniture Store in Aliquippa, Pennsylvania. The memory of those days still has meaning for Ditka.

"Those Little League games helped me a lot," he noted. "They gave me the chance to compete. Winning is everything to a kid. You can't pick up competitiveness in later years if you don't practice it when you're young. I learned how to compete in Little League, how to go after what I wanted, how to strive. And from that time on, I've always enjoyed everything that has to do with competition."

At eleven years old, Chicago Bears coach Mike Ditka was a highly competitive catcher for the Little League team sponsored by Plodnick's furniture store in Alquippa, Pennsylvania.

Doug Flutie's father, Richard (left) attributes the development of Doug's excellent eye and hand coordination to his days in Little League.

Another football figure whose organized sports roots go back to Little League Baseball is **Doug Flutie.** The former Heisman Trophy winner and standout quarterback at Boston college played in the South Beaches Little League in Brevard City, Florida. Doug played second base. His father, Richard, managed his team.

"Doug always had that God-given athletic ability, but it first came out in Little League," Richard Flutie said. "He had excellent eye and hand coordination which was developed as he played Little League. I'll never forget one great play he made. There was a runner on second and one out. Doug went far to his right, fielded a rough hop cleanly, looked at the runner, faked a throw to first, and then dove at the runner off second and tagged him out. I knew than that the kid was something special.

"But Doug wasn't the only one who was special on that Little League scene," Richard Flutie added. "We all took note of another kid one day; the boys from both teams and the adults as well took their eyes off the game to watch this little girl walk across the top of a bar on a metal fence. She looked like a gymnast on a balance beam. Later we learned that she was displaying her specialty. She was Kathy Johnson, and we would all hear a lot about her in the 1984 Olympics."

Kathy Johnson concentrated on her gymnastics and never played Little League Baseball, but that was not that case for another famous Olympian who began his athletic involvement in Little League. **Don Schollander,** who made his mark at the 1964 Olympic Games when he won four gold medals for swimming, recalled how much Little League meant to him.

"I realized how much I enjoyed competition right from the start when I was a second baseman in Little League. The coaches we had on the Alpen Rose Dairy team in Portland, Oregon, made keen competition seem like a good thing. It made for a good time for all of us. Besides teaching me lessons in winning and losing and providing me with lasting friendships, Little League gave me a tremendous amount of enjoyment. And that, after all, is the main reason for playing baseball and for participating in any sport."

Former Heisman Trophy-winner Doug Flutie played in the South Beaches Little League in Brevard City, Florida.

Los Angeles Laker center Kareem Abdul-Jabbar once played Little League Baseball on the opposite coast—in New York City.

Kareem Abdul-Jabbar is a former Little Leaguer who went on to become a legendary figure in the world of professional basketball. The Los Angeles Lakers center once played Little League Baseball on the opposite coast. He was known as Lew Alcindor then, and he lived and played for a team in New York City.

"I remember being presented with our league's sportsmanship award when I was twelve years old," the basketball great recalled. "That was a big thrill; the memory of it is still vivid today. Little League is a great organization. I am proud to have been part of it.

"Our team never won the big game," he continued. "It seems as if we always lost the league championship by one run, and in the All-Star games luck never seemed to be with us. Still, I'll never forget hitting a home run that went over the fence and traveled across two fields to land in the infield of another field. That was my most exciting moment as a Little Leaguer. As a competitor, I was always embarrassed that we never won the big game. But I'll always remember those outstanding times."

"Our team never won the big game," Kareem Abdul-Jabbar recalls of his Little League days.

MALONE
2
SIXERS
10

Actor Kurt Russell recalls playing Little League until he was twelve years old, with his father either coaching or managing all the time.

Little League alumni include show-business celebrities who enjoy reminiscing about the times the audiences they played to sat in the stands and cheered when they got a hit, pitched a strike, or made a good catch for the out.

Actor **Kurt Russell** recalled playing Little League until he was twelve years old, with his father either coaching or managing all the time. "Dad got involved through Dr. Creighton Hale, whom he had known at Dartmouth. And he was a natural since he had been a professional ballplayer. With us, it was a family thing. Girls weren't in Little League back then, but my sister, Jill, used to pitch at batting practice. Then when she grew up, she managed a Little League team in Thousand Oaks, California.

"Dad managed six or seven teams during his seven years with Little League," Russell recalled. "And about eighteen of his players went on to play pro ball. That includes me. I played for a while in the minors before I got hurt.

"I have a favorite Little League memory," the actor added. "It goes back to the time I was nine years old and tried out for the first time. It seemed to me that I was just terrible, but a week later, there I was at my first Little League practice. I was the smallest one in the club. I felt just great being there, being on the team. Except I was kind of disappointed that there were no uniforms for us. I kept wondering when we were going to get them. Finally, the night before opening day, the uniforms arrived. I brought mine home, and Dad helped me put it on.

"I'll never forget the thrill of that moment," Russell smiled. "Here was my dad, an ex-pro player, showing me how to look right in a uniform. There's a correct way to wear them, you know. I looked in the mirror, and I felt I was really something."

Russell reflected on the lessons Little League provided for life. "My coaches emphasized winning. But they also taught us how to lose gracefully and how to cope with disappointments," he said. "My first love was baseball, but the same desire I had to be a ballplayer has now been transferred to being an actor—and in the same spirit as I was taught in Little League."

Tom Selleck is another actor who has good memories of his youthful experiences in Little League. "My father was the president of our Sherman Oaks, California, Pioneer Little League," said Selleck, "so naturally Little League was an important part of our family life. I was a pitcher, and enjoyed some success in that role."

In fact, Selleck was a standout performer, a consistent All-Star who pitched three no-hitters and four one-hitters. "I'm a great advocate of Little League," the actor noted. "I think it's great to be a team player and work with others. In my opinion, parents are making a mistake raising tennis players or golfers. Those sports tend to make young people egotistical and self-centered. When you're on a team, you learn how to get along with other people and accomplish something worthwhile."

On stage Bruce Springsteen often lapses into affectionate reminiscences about playing Little League with the Indians in Freehold, New Jersey.

Rock star **Bruce Springsteen** is today a popular personality who has performed all over the world. From 1959 to 1961, however, Springsteen was a popular Little Leaguer who performed in the Freehold, New Jersey, American League, playing for the Indians. The singer-musician-composer may have come far since those days, but he remains fond of recalling the time when, according to his aunt, Dora Kirby, "Bruce never took his baseball cap off." On stage, in the midst of his concert appearances, Springsteen often lapses into affectionate reminiscences about playing Little League Baseball with the Indians. "Little League had a big impact, a positive impact on my life," says Springsteen.

Fred Rowe, who was Springsteen's Little League manager, remembered how "Bruce made great improvement during his three years in Little League. The best part about him was that he was such a good, nice kid. Everybody liked him. He was an average ballplayer, but a super kid."

A fellow New Jerseyite who played Little League as a youngster and is today a popular show-business personality is actor **Danny DeVito**. Star of the television series *Taxi,* DeVito earned critical acclaim for his performance in the Oscar-winning film *One Flew over the Cuckoo's Nest.* From 1955 to 1957 the talented DeVito played for the Dodgers in the Asbury Park Little League.

There was no Little League in New York City when **Joseph Campanella,** the popular television actor, was a boy. But he has since made up for what he missed in his own youth. As the father of seven sons, Campanella has been coach, manager, and a sponsor in the Toluca Lake Little League in California.

"In New York City when I was growing up in the days before Little League," he said, "the streets belonged to the kids. We lived in them, and we played in them. Rarely did we get into trouble. But after World War II we lost the streets to the cars, and that's when the trouble started. We had no place to play. That's why I think Little League is so great. It gives the kids their place, something to do, and the feeling of accomplishment.

"I really enjoy working with the kids," the genial actor added. "For me it's a great relief from the pressures of work. And as for my own boys, the point I always made with each one as he became a Little Leaguer is that winning or losing is no big deal. Not one of them ever cried when he lost. Not only that, but by the time they finished with practice and did their homework they were ready for bed by ten o'clock or so. They were too tired to even think about getting into trouble. And I'm proud to say they all did well in school.

"The kids in Little League are terrific. The experiences are often unforgettable and hilarious," Campenella continued. "My favorite story is the time during one game when the batter hit to the right fielder, who was standing there as if he was ready to make the catch. Except he never looked up for the ball. He was looking down, and he just stayed that way. Finally we went out to see what was wrong, for it was obvious that he never saw the ball. What had happened was that a gopher had popped his head up out of a hole, and he and the kid were having a staring match."

Campanella admitted to one problem Little League has caused. "It drives my agents crazy," he said. "they're always busy juggling my shooting schedules around practices and games."

As the father of seven sons, actor Joseph Campanella has been coach, manager, and a sponsor in the Toluca Lake Little League in California.

In the *Happy Days* cast was the versatile actor-comedian **Henry Winkler** who delighted audiences with his portrayal of "the Fonz." Little League was a big interest for him. Although Winkler never played himself, he enjoyed watching his stepson Jed in his games. "I was out there every chance I got, a most proud stepparent," Winkler said. "There's a lot to be learned from organized sports like Little League. The basic idea behind the program is wonderful."

Cowboy and California Angels owner Gene Autry once said, "Little League is as American as a good old western movie." And as an all-American institution, Little League can boast of graduates who have gone on to make a profession out of service to America.

William Cohen is today United States senator from his home state of Maine. Perhaps his first distinguished act for his state was when he pitched the first Little League no-hitter in Maine, in 1952. "But that achievement," Senator Cohen said, "is not what I remember most about Little League.

"The most important aspect of Little League Baseball was the sense of discipline and teamwork instilled in me at an early age," the senator continued. "I learned how to cooperate, how to negotiate, how to achieve things as part of a group. These are lessons that are part of my everyday working life as a member of the United States Senate."

There's a lot to be learned from organized sports like Little League," says actor-comedian Henry Winkler.

Thomas J. Downey, congressman from the state of New York, is another elected public official who played Little League Baseball as a boy. "I get a kick out of remembering those days," the congressman said. "One game that stands out in my mind took place when I was ten and was playing infield for Chris' Giants. Chris was a great guy who drove an ice cream truck. He couldn't have had a lot of money, but somehow he cared enough about the kids to sponsor a Little League team.

"On this occasion, we were playing a game that would determine second place," he added. "We were down by fifteen runs, and it looked pretty hopeless. Then suddenly everything went crazy! We got sixteen runs in one inning. We used up four of the opposition's pitchers. Everybody on our team was hitting. I doubled twice in that single inning before they finally got us out. We won the game. Sad to say, we wound up losing the pennant. Still I'll never forget the final score of that incredible game: thirty-two to thirty-one!"

Bill Bradley is a United States senator from the state of New Jersey. Prior to his political career, he was a great player for the New York Knickerbockers, a Rhodes scholar, and a member of the Basketball Hall of Fame. But years before he distinguished himself on the basketball court Bradley was playing Little League Baseball in his native Missouri. "I played on a team in the regional playoffs in Iowa in the mid-1950s," he said. "I was the first baseman. Our team was behind by one run, and it was late in the game. I came to bat and got a walk. For some reason, I took my foot off the base. The first baseman was doing the hidden-ball trick, and he tagged me out. We lost by one run.

"I used to think I couldn't live unless I played baseball," the senator recalled. "And playing it in Little League taught me many valuable things—things like being a good loser and a graceful winner, like putting team effort ahead of personal goals, like putting 100 percent of yourself into every game and practice. For these attitudes and for the many lasting friendships I have made in Little League, I am eternally grateful."

"The purpose of the Little League Baseball program," according to Bowie Kuhn, former baseball commissioner and presently international adviser to Little League Baseball, "is to provide young people with the experience of cooperation in a group setting, the excitement of a competitive situation, and the opportunity to acquire leadership skills. The program also encourages development of the ability to function under pressure."

Kuhn coached Little League Baseball for a brief period when he was a young lawyer in Ridgewood, New Jersey, back in 1965. All four of his children—three sons and a daughter—were in the program. "Watching them play," Kuhn noted, "I realized how Little League helped them develop a sense of self-worth."

The experience of three American astronauts involved in Little League underscores Bowie Kuhn's observations about the program. **Dr. Story Musgrave,** one of seven civilian scientists to qualify as an astronaut in 1967, reflected on the lessons he was able to learn playing Little League Baseball.

"I could write an essay on the contributions, past and present, which Little League Baseball has made in my life. I played in a local league in Massachusetts as a boy. There I learned the concept of training and practice as the means of gaining proficiency. I was exposed to the importance of teamwork and group dynamics—lessons which are so important in our space effort. Ultimately, Little League taught me that life is not all victories. We win a few, but we also lose."

"I used to think I couldn't live unless I played baseball," recalls Sen. Bill Bradley, a Rhodes scholar and member of the Basketball Hall of Fame.

In the early 1980s, Major **James Buchli** of the United States Marine Corps was training with other astronauts at a NASA center in Texas in preparation for a trip into space. As a boy, Buchli played sandlot ball as a left-handed second baseman in New Rockford, North Dakota. "We didn't have Little League there, but I'm glad that my son Jim has had the opportunity to play with the Tigers in Seabrook, Texas," Major Buchli said. "Whenever I was able to get away from classes or flight training, I'd help out. I'd do whatever I could, whether it was coaching, T ball, or working with the kids at the batting machine.

"In a way, there's a parallel between being an astronaut and a Little Leaguer," Buchli added. "The new kids start out every year pretty unsure of themselves. Sometimes they don't even know how to handle a bat. But they develop. I love to watch the joy on their faces when, by the end of the season, they realize they know what they're doing. The Little League program has given them the kind of self-confidence and pride that we astronauts must have."

Shuttle pilot Michael Smith, who was killed in the Challenger explosion, played Little League Baseball in Beaufort, North Carolina.

One of the most decorated pilots in United States history, **Michael Smith** was the pilot of the space shuttle *Challenger*. He was killed along with the other members of his crew in the tragic explosion of the rocket just seventy-three seconds into its flight on January 28, 1986.

Smith was forty years old at his death. In his youth he played in the Little League program with the Beaufort, North Carolina, Elks. As an adult he often commented about how the lessons he learned in Little League, lessons involving discipline and leadership, helped him in later life.

Charlie Hassell, his coach back then, remembered the curly-haired boy: "The thing that sticks out in my mind about Michael is his determination. In everything he did, he was a leader. If we would have had a team captain, undoubtedly it would have been Michael.

"But he never had any aspirations to play pro ball," Hassell added. "All that young man ever wanted to do was fly."

LITTLE LEAGUE BASEBALL CHRONOLOGY

1939

Little League Baseball is founded in Williamsport, Pennsylvania, by Carl Stotz and George and Bert Bebble. . . . A $35 donation is sufficient to purchase uniforms for the first three teams.

1940

Little League expands to include a second league.

1941-1946

During World War II years Little League expands to 12 leagues, all in Pennsylvania.

1947

The Hammonton, New Jersey, Little League becomes first league established outside Pennsylvania. . . . First Little League World Series is won by the Maynard Little League, Williamsport.

The Lycoming Diary Farms teams was the first Little League champion in 1939.

Ray Keyes covered the first Little League game and thousands of games more for the Williamsport Sun-Gazette.

A proud father congratulates his son at the 1953 World Series.

1948

Little League grows to 94 leagues . . . . Lock Haven, Pennsylvania, wins the second Little League World Series.

1949-1950

Little League expands to 307 leagues in the United States . . . . Shortest World Series game—exactly one hour—is played between Hagerstown, Maryland, and Kankakee, Illinois.

1951

First Little League is formed outside the U.S., in British Columbia, Canada . . . . Little League now has 776 programs.

1952

Peter J. McGovern becomes first full-time president of Little League Baseball. . . . Baseball immortal Connie Mack is a visitor to the World Series. . . . Montreal, Canada, becomes the first foreign entry in the World Series. . . . Little League expands to over 1500 programs.

1953

Little League World Series is televised for the first time by CBS and Howard Cosell announces the play-by-play for ABC radio . . . . Lowest possible score for a World Series championship game is recorded when Birmingham, Alabama, defeats Schenectady, New York, 1-0.

1954

Boog Powell, later a member of the Baltimore Orioles, participates for Lakeland, Florida, in the Little League World Series . . . . Cy Young, winningest pitcher in major league history, is a World Series guest. . . . Ken Hubbs, who became the 1962 National League Rookie of the Year with the Chicago Cubs, plays in the Little League World Series for Colton, California . . . . Little League expands to over 3300 leagues.

The cover of the official program for the 1954 World Series.

1955

Cy Young makes his last visit to the Little League World Series before his death in September. . . . Morrisville, Pennsylvania, defeats Delaware, New Jersey, 4-3 in the first extra-inning Little League World Series championship game (7 innings) . . . . Little League is now played in all of the 48 states.

1956

Little League Foundation is created . . . . First World Series perfect game is pitched by Fred Shapiro of Delaware Township, New Jersey . . . . Little League grows to over 4000 leagues.

1957

Monterrey, Mexico, becomes first foreign champion of the Little League World Series . . . . Angel Macias pitches the first perfect game in a World Series championship game.

1958

Monterrey, Mexico becomes first Little League to win consecutive World Series championships . . . . Hector Torres, who later will play in the major leagues, plays for Monterrey . . . . Rick Wise, who also will play in the major leagues, plays for Portland, Oregon, in the World Series.

Cooling off at the 1958 Little League World Series.

1959

The modern protective helmet is developed by Dr. Creighton J. Hale, director of safety research for Little League Baseball. . . . Construction begins on the Little League complex . . . World Series is played for the first time at its present site . . . . Little League now has over 5000 leagues . . . . National Little League Week (second week of June) is proclaimed by President Dwight D. Eisenhower.

1960

First European entry in the Little League World Series is Berlin, Germany . . . . More than 27,400 teams participate in over 5500 Little Leagues.

1961

Senior League Baseball is created for players 13-15 years-old. . . . Former Cleveland Browns quarterback Brian Sipe plays for World Series champion El Cajon, California

1962

Little League Summer Camp opens in Williamsport . . . . Jackie Robinson is inducted into the Baseball Hall of Fame and is a guest at the Little League World Series.

1963

ABC's "Wide World of Sports" televises the Little

Little Leaguers come in all sizes, especially at the 1961 World Series.

League World Series championship game for the first time with Chris Schenkel doing the play-by-play.

1964

Little League Baseball is granted a charter of federal incorporation by the United States Congress . . . . Danny Yacarino pitches a no-hitter and hits a home run to lead Mid Island Little League, Staten Island, New York, over Monterrey, Mexico, 4-0 for the World Series championship.

Safe at home plate as the ball is dropped in the final game of the 1964 World Series.

A proud mom at the 1965 World Series—no more need be said.

1965

Venezuela and Spain are represented in the Little League World Series for the first time.

1966

Little League Baseball's Southern Region Headquarters opens in St. Petersburg, Florida . . . . Longest rain delay during a game in World Series history—one hour and 33 minutes.

1967

West Tokyo, Japan, becomes first Far Eastern team to win Little League World Series championship.

1968

Big League Baseball for players 16-18 years old is started . . . . Darrell Garretson, head of the NBA's Officials Association, is the manager of Garden Grove, California, team in Little League World Series . . . . Turk Schonert, who will become an NFL quarterback, is a member of Garretson's team. . . . Little League now has over 6000 programs.

1969

The Western Region Headquarters of Little League Baseball in San Bernardino, California is opened . . . . Carney Lansford, later a member of the Oakland As, played for Santa Clara, California, in the World Series. . . . Newberry Little League participates in World Series, becoming the first league from the Williamsport area, in the modern era of the World Series play, to be represented.

1970

Canadian Headquarters of Little League opens in Ottawa.

1971

Lloyd McClendon, later to become a member of the Cincinnati Reds, hits five home runs in five at-bats during the World Series for Gary, Indiana. . . . Longest game in World Series is played, taking two hours and 51 minutes (9 innings), between Gary, Indiana, and Tainan, Taiwan . . . . Little League State Center opens in Waco, Texas. . . . The Little League World Series stadium is expanded to increase seating capacity to 9000. . . . The aluminum bat, developed in cooperation with Little League, is first used.

The smiles of victory at the 1966 World Series.

The 1971 World Series champions visit Washington, D.C., and meet with Vice President Spiro Agnew at the White House.

In 1974, the first quints ever played in the Little League—the Prieto brothers from Maracaibo, Venezuela.

1972

Taipei, Taiwan, wins a fourth consecutive World Series championship for the Far East region.

1973

Dr. Creighton J. Hale is elected president of Little League Baseball, the second full-time president in thirty-five years.

1974

Girls participate in Little League as Little League and Senior League Softball programs are created . . . . A Little League state center is opened in Lisle, Illinois.

1975

Baseball Hall of Famers Joe DiMaggio, Ernie Banks, and Bob Gibson are guests at the Little League World Series . . . . Chofu, Japan, wins the World Series title, giving that country its third championship.

1977-1978

Little League grows to include over 6500 Little Leagues for 9-12-year-olds, 2850 Senior Leaguers for 13-15-year-olds, and 1300 Big League programs for 16-18-year-olds . . . . Little League and Senior League Softball teams total over 7400.

1979

Junior League Baseball is created for 13-year-old participants.

1980

Vice President George bush throws out the first pitch for the Little League World Series championship game . . . . Big League Softball is started for players 16-18 years old.

1981

For the second consecutive year the Belmont Heights Little League, Tampa, Florida, plays in the championship game of the Little League World Series, losing for the second time by a total of three runs to the Far East.

1982

The Peter J. McGovern Little League Museum opens in South Williamsport on the Little League Headquarters complex. . . . Kirkland, Washington, defeats Pu-tzu Town, Taiwan, 6-0 before a World Series record crowd of 40,000.

A Little Leaguer from Long Island, New York, poses for the traditional photo.

1983

Baseball Commissioner Bowie Kuhn throws the ceremonial first pitch for the Little League World Series championship game and musical superstar Chuck Mangione plays the Dominican Republic national anthem.

1984

Seoul, Korea, wins that country's first Little League World Series championship, defeating Altamonte Springs, Florida, 6-2. . . . Peter J. McGovern, Little League board chairman for over 30 years, dies June 30.

1985

For the first time ABC carries the Little League World Series championship game live on "Wide World of sports." . . . DUGOUT, the Disney-created mascot of Little League Baseball, is introduced at the World Series . . . . For the first time in baseball history ABC mounts a microminiature camera on the mask of the home-plate umpire.

1986

Baseball Commissioner Peter Ueberroth makes his first visit to the Little League World Series for the championship game . . . . Bill Shea, president of the Little League Foundation and the man for whom New York's Shea Stadium is named, throws the ceremonial first pitch.

1987

40th anniversary of the Little League World Series is celebrated . . . . The 1947 Little League World Series champions, the Maynard Little League of Williamsport, are reunited on the field before the championship game . . . . Former New York Mets pitching great and Little League graduate Tom Seaver tosses the first pitch.

The 1986 World Series championship battery celebrates.

Orel Hershiser signs autographs at the 1988 World Series.

1988

Mr. and Mrs. Orel Hershiser III are honored as Little League Parents of the Year . . . . Tom Seaver is named as the first inductee to the Peter J. McGovern Museum's Hall of Fame for Distinguished Little League Graduates . . . . Plans are announced for the development of the first Little League Friendship Field in China . . . . Ground is broken in Indianapolis, Indiana, for construction of a Central Region Center.

1989

The fiftieth anniversary of Little League Baseball is celebrated with many events and special programs, including the publication of *Growing up at Bat.*

EPILOGUE

From the windy chill of early spring into the sun-kissed days of summer, the ceremony has repeated itself through a half-century of changing fashions, carping critics, the competition of other sports and programs, and political upheaval. None of these has stopped the ceremony: registration, tryout, getting the team cap and uniform, the big parade, the endless practice, the games of summer.

Little League Baseball is a montage of sights, sounds, memories: fields swept clean, dirt raked, grass mown, the arriving vans and bikes and station wagons, the lawn chairs lining the periphery of the diamond, the jugs of juice and collections of sun visors, the tumbled rush of the players—graceful and awkward—in their uniforms of blue or white or gray or red, with the team names Dodgers or Cardinals or Yankees or Royal boldly emblazoned on the shirt fronts and the sponsors' names—Lundy's Lumber or Smolnick's Furniture or Morton's Army-Navy or Pants Patio—sedately stitched on the shirts' backs.

Then the eager anticipation, the ping of ball against bat, the smack of ball into glove. And the familiar shouts: "Atta boy!," "Good eye!," "Go for it!," "Let's get something going!," "Nice swing!," "Stay with it!"

Now into its second half-century, Little League Baseball is a glorious ceremony of summer for millions of children all over the world.

19____ to 19____

Team Photo

Team Sponsor ______________________________

Uniform Colors ______________________________

MY PHOTOS

My Teammates:

1st Base ________________________________

2nd Base ________________________________

Shortstop ________________________________

3rd Base ________________________________

Right Field ________________________________

Center field ________________________________

Left Field ________________________________

Catcher ________________________________

Pitcher ________________________________

Coaches ________________________________

Won-Lost Record

1 9 _____ _____—_____

1 9 _____ _____—_____

1 9 _____ _____—_____

Best play ________________________________

Best game ________________________________

INDEX

ABOUT THE AUTHOR

Harvey Frommer is one of America's most prolific and versatile authors, with twenty-six books and hundreds of articles to his credit. A Ph.D. in communications, Frommer has been cited in the *Congressional Record* and honored by the New York state legislature as a sports historian. His most recent books include *Red on Red: The Autobiography of Red Holzman* (Bantam) and *Throwing Heat: The Autobiography of Nolan Ryan* (Doubleday).